Amrita of Eloquence

Amrita *of* Eloquence
A Biography of Khenpo Karthar Rinpoche

A translation of *Amrita of Eloquence, Medicine for Our Faith: A Brief Biography of Our Great Holy Guide, the Learned and Accomplished Khenpo Karma Tarchin*

Written by Lama Karma Drodül
Translated by Lama Yeshe Gyamtso

KTD Publications, Woodstock, New York

Published by: KTD Publications
335 Meads Mountain Road
Woodstock, NY 12498, USA
www.KTDPublications.org

Distributed by: www.NamseBangdzo.com

© 2009 Karma Triyana Dharmachakra
ISBN 978-1-934608-05-0
Printed in the USA on acid-free paper

Contents

The Karmapa

༄༅། །དང་ཆོ་མིའི་འཇིག་རྟེན་དུ་ཡུན་རིང་འཆོ་སྲིད་བྱས་པའི་རིན་བབས་སྷ་ཧྲང་མི་རེ་ཌོ་རེ་ནས་སྐྱི་ཆོ་གས་
བདེ་ཐབས་ཀྱི་ལེགས་སྐྱེས་རེ་ཕུལ་ཐུབ་དགོས་པ་ནི་ལྷན་སྐྱེས་ཀྱི་འགན་འཁྲི་ཡིན་ལ། ད་ཐེངས་མཁན་པོ་
གར་ཐར་རིན་པོ་ཆེས་རྒྱལ་དབང་སྐུ་གོང་མའི་དགོངས་པ་གཞིར་བཟུང་གིས་ལོ་རྟོག་མའི་རིང་ཐར་ཐུབ་ཡུལ་
གྱུ་ཀྲམས་སུ་ནང་ཆོས་དང་སྒྱིལ་ཆེད་འབད་བརྩོན་བླ་ལྷག་གནང་བ་ནི་རེས་སུ་མ་ཆད་པའི་སྐྱེ་འགྲོ་གང་མང་
ཞིག་གི་འདི་ཕྱིའི་བདེ་དོན་དོམ་དེ་ཡིན་གཤིས་བསྔགས་འོས་སུ་གྱུར་ཅིང་། གང་གི་མཛད་ཕྲིན་རྣམས་ཀུན་དོན་
གྲུབ་ཀྱིས་ཡིག་ཕོག་ཏུ་བཀོད་པ་དེས་ཀྱང་དགོས་འབྱུང་གི་ལོ་རྒྱལ་རྩད་འཆོལ་བྱེད་པ་དང་། ལེགས་སྐྱེལ་ཞེས་
འགོག་གི་ཐབས་གྲུབ་མོ་སྐྱུབ་བྱེད་པར་གལ་འགགས་ཆེ་བའི་ཐར་ཕོགས་འབྱུང་ངེས་ཡིན་ཕྱིར་ཐོས་ནས་ཡི་
རང་བྱ་བ་དང་ཆབས་ཅིག་གང་ཅིའི་ལེགས་ལམ་རྣམས་ཡར་ངོའི་ཟླ་ལྟར་འཕེལ་བའི་སྨོན་ལམ་ཡོད།

གཀྱ་ལ་ཨོ་རྒྱན་ཕྲིན་ལས་རྡོ་རྗེས། ནང་ལོ་ ༢༥༥༢ སྤྱི་ལོ་ ༢༠༠༨ ཟླ་བ་ ༡༢ པའི་ཆེས་ ༢

Foreword
The Gyalwang Karmapa, Ogyen Trinley Dorje

The price of living a long life in this world of ours is our duty to be able to offer some contribution to everyone's welfare. Based on the intentions of the previous Gyalwang Karmapa, Khenpo Karthar Rinpoche has for many years engaged in extraordinary efforts to spread Buddhism throughout many countries in the East and West. Since by doing so he has truly caused the present and future happiness of many beings, he is worthy of praise. Karma Drodül's written description of Khenpo Rinpoche's deeds is based on factual accounts of the events described. This is definitely a significant contribution to our resources for the increase of goodness and the prevention of wrongdoing. I therefore rejoice in this, and make the aspiration that every aspect of goodness may increase like the waxing moon.

Written by Karmapa Ogyen Trinley Dorje on December 26th, 2008, in the Buddhist Year 2552.

Traleg Rinpoche and Khenpo Rinpoche, near Thrangu Monastery, Kham, East Tibet, 2004.

Preface
The Ninth Traleg Kyabgön Rinpoche

It is my great pleasure to introduce this excellent biography of Khenpo Karthar Rinpoche. Traditionally, a Tibetan master is supposed to possess three essential qualities: extensive learning, impeccable moral character, and a kindly disposition (khe tsun zang sum). Khenpo Karthar Rinpoche possesses all three in abundance.

Khenpo Rinpoche was born in 1924 as a very gifted child. Even at a very early age, his spiritual inclinations were evident for all to see. Khenpo Rinpoche, along with Khenchen Thrangu Rinpoche, went through extensive study under the guidance of the most venerable Khenpo Lodro Rapsel, at Thrangu Monastery in Kham, Yushu. Khenpo Rinpoche subsequently went on to pursue further studies for many years, especially at Buxa, where many of the greatest khenpos and geshes from all traditions were congregated.

Khenpo Rinpoche's extensive learning is clearly exemplified by his complete ease in discussing everything from the finer points of Madhyamaka to tantric philosophy and ritual practices. Rinpoche's impeccable morality is exemplified in the way he has followed the strict monastic code of behavior for all his ordained life. No one can fault Rinpoche's moral character or adherence to the life of a fully ordained bhikshu or his keeping of the vows and commitments to the tantric teachings and practices. Rinpoche's kindly disposition is exemplified by his great humility despite his formidable learning and outstanding intellect and by how he has worked tirelessly for the dharma and for the realization of His Holiness Karmapa's vision in America. It can also be seen in the way he has patiently guided his many students through their dharma study and practices and his intimate involvement with them through providing counsel, practical encouragement, and even worldly advice.

The Kagyu tradition and Buddhism in general would be considerably poorer without Khenpo Rinpoche's extraordinary dedication and tireless effort. Lama Karma Drodül has done a tremendous service to the Kagyu tradition by compiling this much-needed biography of this great modern-day Tibetan master. As it is said in the traditional teachings, "Masters of this stature are becoming rarer than a star in the midday summer sky." Biographies of great lamas have always been read as a source of inspiration and I have absolutely no doubt this biography will bring definite inspiration to everyone who reads it.

Preface
The Ninth Khenchen Thrangu Rinpoche

Throughout his many years of teaching, Khenpo Karthar Rinpoche has consistently demonstrated his reliability and his goodness, the characteristics of a genuine spiritual friend. He always shows great love and affection for his students. I have known him ever since we were young monks in Thrangu Monastery in Tibet. In 1959, we fled together from Tibet. I am very pleased that this account of his life is now being published in English.

Lama Karma Drodül's first time translating for Rinpoche, Pawo Ling, Karme Ling Retreat Center, Delhi, New York, 2007.

From the Author

First of all I would like to say that I am really happy that I was able to write a namtar of Rinpoche and especially I am very happy that the namtar was translated into English through the kindness of Lama Yeshe Gyamtso. I also thank Maureen and all those people who worked to publish the book. I feel I am finally able to show a little good work for the students of Rinpoche. I also pray that my second book, *Kham Masters*, which was also told by Rinpoche, will soon be translated into English and published. I would like to dedicate all the merit for the long life of our kind guru Khenpo Karthar Rinpoche. May his dharma activities flourish. May this cause to arise unshakable devotion that is like amrita for the path. May this cause all war, strife, and sickness to cease, and bring peace to our world.

Lama Karma Drodül

Lama Yeshe Gyamtso translating for Rinpoche, Ten-Day Teaching, Karma Triyana Dharmachakra, Woodstock, New York, 2002.

Translator's Introduction

Amrita of Eloquence: A Biography of Khenpo Karthar Rinpoche is a translation of *Amrita of Eloquence, Medicine for Our Faith: A Brief Biography of Our Great Holy Guide, the Learned and Accomplished Khenpo Karma Tarchin.* The biography was written in 2005 by Lama Karma Drodül, Khenpo Karthar Rinpoche's nephew.

There is no need for me to write here at length about the value and function of biographies like this one; our author explains these fully and provides quotations from the Buddha and other teachers to support his statements. His argument for the importance of such biographies is elegant in its simplicity. Studying the life of one's guru brings devotion, and devotion brings awakening. There is nothing I need add to what Lama Karma has written.

As for the subject of this biography, Lama Karma describes Khenpo Rinpoche and his life with lyrical beauty, devotion, affection, and humor. He captures and vividly portrays Rinpoche's personality. There is nothing for me to add to this either.

I do, however, have a few things to say about our author, Lama Karma Drodül. Born in 1974 in eastern Tibet, Lama Karma became a monk of Thrangu Monastery at the age of thirteen and received full ordination at twenty. He came to the United States in 1997 and has been his uncle's attendant ever since. He has now also completed two three-year retreats at the Karme Ling Retreat Center in Delhi, New York.

Although Lama Karma writes disparagingly of himself at every opportunity in his book, I caution the reader not to believe anything he writes about himself. He is one of the kindest, brightest, and most engaging people I know. Although it is impossible for me to see inside his mind, his lack of selfishness leads me to conclude that his spiritual state is one worthy of admiration.

I mention this because, as you will see, it is customary for Tibetan writers of biographies to disparage themselves while praising their subject. This is not merely for the sake of contrast. The reason for this custom is that it reminds the reader that humility is essential at every moment of the spiritual journey. We all know this, but many of us seem to forget it from time to time. Books like this and writers like Lama Karma Drodül can help to remind us.

Lama Karma wrote his book as an exercise in devotion, a labor of love. In its original Tibetan it has been published by Karme Ling Retreat Center and circulated around the world. It has been translated with the author's permission, as well as that of its subject, so that Khenpo Rinpoche's many disciples can study their guru's life and come at least a bit closer to being like him.

I must thank both Khenpo Karthar Rinpoche and Lama Karma Drodül for patiently answering my interminable questions while I was translating this biography, and Peter van Deurzen and Maureen McNicholas for both making it possible to publish it and making it a visually beautiful book.

Lama Yeshe Gyamtso

Karma Triyana Dharmachakra, ca. 1979.

From the Publisher

It brings great joy to our hearts to have this namtar of our precious guru Khenpo Karthar Rinpoche and we wish to express our sincere appreciation to Rinpoche for his life and teachings that have touched all of us students with his kindness and blessings. It is a rare and fortunate opportunity to learn about Rinpoche's life in Tibet before he came to this country. We are both immeasurably humbled and immeasurably inspired by our guru's life story. Thank you Rinpoche.

This precious biography of Khenpo Karthar Rinpoche was originally published as *Amrita of Eloquence, Medicine for Our Faith: A Brief Biography of Our Great Holy Guide, the Learned and Accomplished Khenpo Karma Tarchin*, written by Rinpoche's nephew Lama Karma Drodül at the request of Lodrö Nyima Rinpoche for Thrangu Monastery in East Tibet, 2005. Thank you Lodrö Nyima Rinpoche for requesting this namtar.

Khenpo Rinpoche has now allowed us to translate his namtar into English, which Lama Yeshe Gyamtso has done. The English title is: *Amrita of Eloquence, A Biography of Khenpo Karthar Rinpoche*. Thank you Lama Karma Drodül for writing

His Holiness the Sixteenth Gyalwang Karmapa, USA, ca. 1977.

this namtar so beautifully and thank you Lama Yeshe Gyamtso for translating the namtar with such care.

Our sincere thanks to Florence Wetzel for her invaluable editorial work, to Stephanie Colvey for preparing the numerous photographs in the book, and to Sandy Hu and Jigme Nyima for their generous support.

Most photographs found in this book are from the Karma Triyana Dharmachakra (KTD) archives and the Karme Ling archives. We do not know all who were responsible for the wonderful photographs we used in this book. We offer our gratitude and apologies to each of you. We also are not certain of the exact dates for some of the photographs, although we can give approximate dates. We apologize for this as well.

We thank Tim Wolf for the photographs on pages xiv and xxii, Stephanie Colvey for those on pages vi and 98, Seichi Tsusumi for the photograph on page 127, Andrea Barrist-Stern for the photograph on page 155, Michael Erlewine for page 82, from the KTD archives: Naomi Schmidt, Tim Wolf, Seichi Tsusumi, Basia Coulter, Sharon Mumby, and from the Karme Ling archives: Lama Karma Drodül, his brother Karma Drime, Lama Tsultrim Gyaltsen, Lama Karma Lodrö, Lama Ani Lodrö, and Ani Karuna. We thank you all.

Maureen McNicholas and Peter van Deurzen

Ten-Day Teaching, Karma Triyana Dharmachakra, 2000.

This namtar is dedicated to the long life
of our kind guru, Khenpo Karthar Rinpoche.

May his dharma activities flourish.
May this cause to arise unshakable devotion,
Which is like amrita for the path.
May this cause all war, strife,
And sickness to cease,
And bring peace to our world.

Amrita of Eloquence
A Biography of Khenpo Karthar Rinpoche

A translation of *Amrita of Eloquence, Medicine for Our Faith: A Brief Biography of Our Great Holy Guide, the Learned and Accomplished Khenpo Karma Tarchin*

Thrangu Monastery after the 1959 invasion, Kham, East Tibet, 2006.
Toward the top of the mountain on the right is the Vairochana retreat house called the
Mandala of Chakrasamvara by Mipham Rinpoche, who did retreat here. Also, this is
where the Second Jamgön Rinpoche passed away. The large building in the back, at the
foot of the mountain, is the shedra. The low building at the far right is the three-year
retreat. The large building toward the foreground is the main hall of the monastery.

Part One
Virtue in the Beginning

Thrangu Monastery before the 1959 Chinese invasion, East Tibet, 1930s.

Virtue in the Beginning

NAMO GURU!

With rays of wisdom's sunlight you dissolve
    our dark folly into space.
Your kind compassion reaches all beings, our
    mothers.
Your power conquers the four maras and places
    beings on the path to freedom.[1]
I bow devotedly with my three gates to the
    perfect Buddha.[2]

You bravely uphold the golden-handled white
    parasol of the Victor's teachings,
Tradition and realization, teaching and practice.
Especially, you illuminate the teachings of
    accomplishment.

1. The four maras are devaputramara, the mara that is the child of the gods; skandhamara, the mara of the aggregates; kleshamara, the mara of kleshas; and death. In the most general terms, a mara is anything that impedes the achievement of full awakening.

2. The three gates are body, speech, and mind.

3. A threefold guru is one who possesses the three vows: the pratimoksha or individual liberation vow of the common vehicle, the bodhisattva vow of the mahayana, and the samaya of the vajrayana.

4. The six realms or six states are hell, the hungry ghost realm, the animal realm, the human realm, the jealous god realm, and the joyous god realm.

5. Shuddhodana was the name of the Buddha's father.

The most common list of the Buddha's twelve deeds is:
1) Departure from the Tushita heaven
2) Conception
3) Birth
4) Youthful play
5) Experience of married life
6) Renunciation of the home
7) Austerity
8) Journey to the site of awakening
9) Defeat of all maras
10) Buddhahood
11) Teaching
12) Parinirvana or passing away.

The dharmakaya (the dharma body) can be thought of

Threefold guru, I venerate you as the ornament of
    my crown.[3]

Kindly, as if they were your children, you lead the
    vast six realms,
Our parents, on the path to freedom.[4]
Especially, you guide those from borderlands.
I bow from my heart to the great beings of all
    traditions.

Among the traditions of the Victor's teachings from
    the land of snow-covered mountains,
This lineage of accomplishment — the Kagyu,
    beings' protectors —
Emphasizes devotion as the essence of practice.
I will therefore recount the life of my guru.

Led by those words — the casting of flowers of veneration with hands of faith, and my promise to write — I will begin this biography.

Our kind teacher, the peerless son of Shuddhodana, performed the twelve deeds for others and extensively turned the vast and profound dharmachakras without straying from the dharmakaya.[5]

Because of him, many holy beings have appeared in many places. They are all emanations of the teacher himself. Their skillful deeds are beyond the grasp of the intellect. In order to tame individual beings, they have appeared and continue to appear as monarchs, brahmins, and bhikshus; as men and women; even as bridges, ships, and other things.[6] In these ways they ripen and liberate vast numbers of beings. It has been taught that during evil, decadent times they will appear as spiritual friends.

From the *River Current Sutra*:

> During the final five hundred years
> I will appear as spiritual friends.[7]
> Recognize them as me.
> Give rise to devotion for them.

From the *Great Drum Sutra*:

> Do not mourn me, Ananda!
> I will return in the future
> As emanated spiritual friends.
> They will help you all.

Our time is one of extreme degeneracy. The Buddha never said that for ordinary beings like me, tormented by the chronic illness of karma, the guru would appear with an ushnisha on his head and wheels on the soles of his feet, or with the other marks and signs, or able to fly in the sky and pass through solid earth, or with many faces and hands.[8] It is rather taught that one must depend upon a guru who accords with one's own level and path.

5. (continued) as the awakened mind of a buddha. Dharmachakras (dharma wheels) are the teachings of a buddha.

6. Brahmins are members of the priestly caste of India. Bhikshus are Buddhist monks.

7. The Buddha predicted that his teachings would remain in this world for five thousand years, divided into ten periods of five hundred years each. Each of these periods is more spiritually degraded than the previous one, so the final five hundred years will be a time in which only the empty shell and outer form of Buddhism will remain.

8. An ushnisha is the crown protrusion at the top of a buddha's head. The ushnisha and the wheels on the palms of the hands and soles of the feet are two of thirty-two marks and eighty signs found on the body of every buddha.

From the *Ornament of Liberation*:

> A beginner is not capable of depending upon a buddha or a bodhisattva on the great levels. Depend, therefore, upon a spiritual friend who is an ordinary person. When your karmic obscurations have been mostly purified, depend upon a spiritual friend who is a bodhisattva on the great levels. When you reach the greater path of accumulation, you will be able to depend upon a spiritual friend who is a nirmanakaya buddha. When you reach the great levels, you will be able to depend upon a spiritual friend who is a sambhogakaya.[9] But if you ask who among these four is the kindest, it is the spiritual friend who is an ordinary person. As beginners we live in the darkness of our own karma and kleshas.[10] We cannot depend upon the higher spiritual friends; we cannot even see their faces! Nevertheless when we meet a spiritual friend who is an ordinary person, the path is illuminated by the beacon of his teaching. Because of him, we will later meet the higher spiritual friends; but of them all, the spiritual friend who is an ordinary person is the kindest.

9. A nirmanakaya buddha is a buddha who appears to ordinary beings, as did the historical buddha. A sambhogakaya buddha only appears to other buddhas and to bodhisattvas.

Nirmanakaya means "emanation body." *Sambhogakaya* means "body of perfect enjoyment."

10. Kleshas are negative emotions such as hatred.

The attributes of a spiritual friend are extensively taught in all sutras and tantras. In brief, from the *Bodhicharyavatara*:

> A spiritual friend is always
> Learned in the mahayana

And never gives up the supreme discipline
Of a bodhisattva even at the cost of his life.

In particular, the following are taught to be the necessary attributes of a guru who teaches the instructions
of the vajrayana of secret mantra:

He must have received empowerment, remain in
    samaya, and be extremely tranquil.
He must understand the tantras of ground, path,
    and fruition.
He must have achieved all the signs of approach
    and accomplishment.[11]
With a mind liberated through realization, he
    must aim only at others' benefit with
    immeasurable compassion.
He must have few activities and diligently
    contemplate dharma.
He must have great sadness and encourage it
    in others.
He must be skillful and have the blessing of his
    lineage.
If you depend upon someone like that, siddhi
    will come quickly.[12]

The possession of all these attributes by our holy guru
can be understood from the following biography, so I
will not say more about it here.

    We, his disciples, have wandered throughout
beginningless samsara, overpowered by karma and

11. Approach and accomplishment are two stages in the process of accomplishing a yidam (a meditation deity).

12. Siddhi is attainment, and can refer to both the supreme attainment of awakening and the lesser attainment of magical abilities.

13. *Bodhichitta*, the "mind of awakening," refers both to the intention to achieve perfect awakening for all beings' benefit, and to the actual achievement of that awakening.

14. A vidyadhara, an awareness-holder, is a master practitioner of vajrayana.

15. Rangjung Rigpe Dorje (1924-1981) was the Sixteenth Gyalwang Karmapa. The Karmapa is both an emanation of Avalokita, the bodhisattva who embodies the compassion of all buddhas, and the presence in one person of the activity of all buddhas.

16. Vajradhara is the Buddha as a teacher of tantra. In vajrayana practice one identifies one's guru with Vajradhara.

kleshas. He is the guide who opens our eyes to right and wrong. For those of us tormented by the chronic illness of bad samsaric karma, he is a great physician. For those of us drowning in the vast ocean of suffering and wailing with desperation, he is a great captain who brings us to the dry land of liberation. For those of us trapped in the darkness of the bardo of possibility and wandering through its terrifying passage, he is a great hero who shines the light of emptiness and compassion and frees us from danger.

He has watered the good soil of the outer pratimoksha's pure morality with the moisture of bodhichitta, the inner unity of emptiness and compassion.[13] His fine fruit of a vidyadhara has ripened secretly and causes the branches of his deeds and activity to bow with its weight.[14] In particular, the great lord of the doctrine of the accomplishment lineage, the appearance of the supremely noble Avalokita as a master, the lord of the victors whose name is difficult to utter, Gyalwang Karmapa Palden Rangjung Yeshe Rigpe Dorje, blessed our guru with his three secrets, bestowed upon him the title "Lord of Dharma," and sent him to the United States of America as his representative.[15]

Our holy lord of dharma, whose kindness to us is immeasurable, is the all-pervasive lord of all mandalas, Vajradhara, appearing as a spiritual friend.[16] It is difficult to utter his name, but if called by the names he bears through timely auspiciousness, he is the lord of refuges, the peerless Khenpo Sönam Gyurmay or Khenpo Karma Tarchin Rinpoche.

The oceans of deeds of his three secrets would be difficult for even great bodhisattvas to fathom.[17] It need not be said that they are beyond the estimation of someone like me who is both unintelligent and trapped in a tornado of karma.[18] However this holy being has been so kind to me in bestowing empowerment, transmission, and instruction that even if I sliced my body into pieces, weighed it on a balance, and offered it to him I could never repay his kindness. Although I lack any of the qualifications the writer of his biography or even a disciple should have — such as discernment and confidence in my meditation experience — I am stirred by my meager devotion. I will write briefly of the main events of his outer life, just as I have heard them described. I will neither exaggerate nor conceal anything. I set about this with the best of intentions. I hope that what I write here may serve as healing medicine for his disciples who have eyes widened with pure perception, and that it will also remind me of how much my kind guru has done for us.

Jamgön Kongtrul wrote:

> The word *namtar* is a translation of the Sanskrit *vimoksha*, which means "complete freedom" or "complete liberation."[19] In the case of a lesser person with pure faith, it refers to the story of how they

17. The three secrets are the body, speech, and mind of an awakened being. They are called "secret" because their qualities are inconceivable to ordinary beings.

18. Throughout his book, Karma Drodül refers to himself with extreme modesty. This is a traditional way for the writer of such books to demonstrate the necessity of modesty on the spiritual path.

19. *Namtar* is the Tibetan word for the biography or hagiography of a holy being. Its etymology is explained in this quotation.

achieved complete freedom from lower states of existence. In the case of an intermediate person with pure renunciation, it refers to the story of how they achieved complete freedom from the ocean of samsara. In the case of a superior person with pure benevolence, it refers to the story of how they achieved complete liberation from both existence and tranquility. The purpose in telling such stories is to cause those who see or hear them to give rise to all or any of the three types of faith.[20] Giving rise to faith will awaken their innate potential and plant within them the seed of freedom.

20. The three types of faith are the faith of awe, the faith of aspiration, and the faith of belief.

From the sutras:

> Ananda, apply yourself to faith. That is the tathagata's prayer.[21]

21. *Tathagata* is a synonym for "Buddha."

And:

> Faith produces virtue like a mother giving birth.

And:

> For people without faith
> Virtues will not arise,
> Just as a burnt seed
> Cannot produce a living sprout.

This is taught in many sutras and tantras. Also someone who even casually reflects upon the life of a holy being and explains it so that others can understand it has planted a seed of virtue by giving rise to faith and devotion, even if they do so only once. It is certain that they will greatly benefit. This is because holy beings have the intention and benevolent aspiration that all contact with them be beneficial.

Especially, the peerless Dakpo Kagyu places particular emphasis on devotion.[22] The ocean of past Kagyu siddhas all achieved the supreme siddhi of mahamudra in one life through the sudden transference to them of the blessings of the three secrets of a guru from this lineage.[23] All of them achieved this by giving rise to unfabricated devotion for the lives of their gurus and then, through the medium of prayer, mixing their minds with their gurus' minds and meditating. Studying the lives of one's root and lineage gurus is a genuine cause of authentic devotion. I shall therefore write here of the major events in the outer life of my great and kind guru.

The first part, "Virtue in the Beginning," was the above veneration, promise to write, and introduction.

22. The Dakpo Kagyu is the lineage of Gampopa, who is also called Dakpo Rinpoche. The Dakpo Kagyu has twelve main branches, one of which is the Karma Kagyu, Khenpo Rinpoche's lineage.

23. Mahamudra, the great seal, is the principal meditation practice of the Kagyu tradition. The word *mahamudra* is also used to refer to the result of such meditation and to the nature that is the basis for such meditation. A siddha is someone who has achieved siddhi.

Karma Triyana Dharmachakra before construction of the new building, 2000.

Part Two
Virtue in the Middle

Students offered the Gampopa Gateway, where all will pass to enter the new building, as a gift to Rinpoche — to honor Rinpoche and to assist with fund-raising for
the new building. Ten-Day Teaching, Karma Triyana Dharmachakra, 2007.

The second part, "Virtue in the Middle," is the actual biography. I will divide this into twelve chapters, corresponding in number to the Buddha's twelve deeds, that will describe twelve aspects of our guru's greatness.

Gampopa, Dakpo Rinpoche, 1079-1153.

Chapter One
The Greatness of His Birthplace

Birthplace of Khenpo Karthar Rinpoche, Rapshul, Kham, East Tibet. Rinpoche's younger sister, Tsekyi Tsomo, is standing on the spot where Rinpoche was born on the twenty-ninth day of the second month in the Year of the Wood Mouse, 1924; photograph taken 2005.

The Greatness of His Birthplace

The field of activity of Shakyamuni, the fourth buddha of this fortunate kalpa, includes one billion
Jambudvipas.[24] The center of Jambudvipa in our world
is Vajrasana in India. To the north of it is a land in
which the mahayana dharma and its adherents prolif-
erate. That land, the field of activity of Arya
Avalokita, is the realm of snow-covered mountains
called Tibet. Its territory is said to include the three
regions of Ngari in the west, the four regions of Ü and
Tsang in the middle, and the six regions of Kham in
the east. One of these six is called Drida Zalmogang.

Within it is the beautiful region of Ga, in which
there are many self-arisen sacred images. In the south
of that populous region is an area called Rapshul.
People there naturally practice the ten virtues, and
both men and women there have great faith in

24. Shakyamuni
is the name of the
historical buddha.
He is said to have
been the fourth of
one thousand
buddhas who will
appear in this
world. A kalpa is
the duration of a
world. The part of
the world in which
he appeared is
called Jambudvipa
by Buddhists. He
is said to have
simultaneously
appeared in the
corresponding
parts of one billion
inhabited worlds.

25. The ten virtues are saving lives instead of taking lives; being generous instead of stealing; being chaste instead of promiscuous; telling the truth instead of lying; promoting harmony instead of discord; speaking kindly instead of abusively; speaking meaningfully instead of gossiping; being content instead of coveting what belongs to others; being benevolent instead of malicious; and believing in the truth instead of what is untrue.

26. The eight attributes are that the water is sweet, cool, soft, light, transparent, clean, pleasant to the throat, and beneficial to the stomach.

27. The six syllables are OM MANI PADME HUM, the mantra of the bodhisattva Avalokita.

dharma.[25] Its meadows are lushly green. Wild herbivores such as deer and gazelles move about freely and playfully, safe from harm. Birds, including swans and geese, give forth their sweet calls and cavort in the sky. Flowers, trees, and sweet herbs spring spontaneously from the earth, waving gracefully in gentle, pure breezes that are as melodious as song. The white rocky peaks of the mountains there are so high they seem to pierce the sky. Their grassy slopes gleam like turquoise. The mountains are like white snow lionesses shaking their turquoise manes. There are dense forests filled with trees with beautiful branches covered by white and red flowers, soft green leaves, and all sorts of fruit. The water of the Dzachu River is clean and cool. It appears blue as it flows through the mountains and valleys. This water is the pure and refreshing drink of all the people and animals there. The lakes there are filled with water of eight attributes.[26] These blue, swirling lakes are surrounded by vast meadows covered by flowers and grass. On the lakes live divine birds with long gentle calls, such as cranes and ducks. They live in freedom, spreading their resplendent wings.

The young, rosy-cheeked herders, devoted to virtue, plant the seed of freedom in all who hear them by singing OM MANI PADME HUM. The white-haired elders devote their lives to the accumulation of virtue, with prayer wheels in their hands and the dharmic sound of the six syllables issuing from their mouths.[27]

They are generous both in their offerings to holy fields
of accumulation and in their giving to the poor. Even
the wild, strong young men there carefully observe
the results of actions and are stalwart in friendship
and enmity. Because people there live virtuously,
both people and livestock are rarely menaced by dis-
ease or demons. Horses, livestock, goats, and sheep
adorn the surrounding mountainsides. The neighing
of horses, lowing of livestock, and bleating of sheep
make one powerless to resist an upsurge of joy from
the depths of one's heart.

The nomads' tents there are decorated with flags
inscribed with scripture such as the "Tara Praises,"
planting the seed of liberation in all who see them.
Monasteries of all four lineages preside over all parts
of the area, placing beings, our past mothers, on the
great path to higher rebirth and liberation.[26] In isolat-
ed, pleasant mountain retreats, yogins and yoginis
cultivate experience and realization and ceaselessly
enjoy, free from craving, the magical display of the
bliss of pliancy.[29] Their realization songs burst forth
spontaneously from the expanse of awareness. All
who hear them are led to the royal city of liberation.
These are the unique, self-arisen attributes of Tibet in
general and the virtues of Rapshul in particular.

During the life of the Fourteenth Gyalwang
Karmapa, Tekchok Dorje, the single embodiment of
all the victors' activity, there lived a treasure revealer
called Geri Chögyal Dorje.[30] He practiced in a place

28. The four lineages are the Kagyu, Nyingma, Sakya, and Geluk

29. Yogins and yoginis are male and female medi-tators. Pliancy is the state of body and mind that results from tran-quility meditation.

30. Treasure revealers are visionary masters who reveal and disseminate dhar-ma teachings that were previously concealed in order to be preserved for future use.

called Anye Nyengyal. That treasure revealer's
rebirth, Lama Tapkay of Ayung Monastery, practiced
in a place called Kogyal Ngangma. Near both these
sites is a place called Makhoda, which was the birthplace of our holy guru.

> In the sky of benevolent bodhichitta
> A young moon with all the marks and signs is
>   about to be born!
> This was the eager praise of all the gods and
>   people of this world
> When, crown-jewel of all beings, your victorious
>   birth was imminent.

Chapter Two
The Greatness of the Time and Signs of His Birth

With Lodrö Nyima Tulku Rinpoche, Taiwan, 1997.

The Greatness of the Time and Signs of His Birth

Rinpoche was born on a day sacred to the dharma-pala Mahakala in the spring of 1924, during the Great Aspiration Prayer Festival of Ranyak Monastery.[31] At sunrise on the twenty-ninth day of the second month of the Tibetan calendar, his mother went to fetch water. As soon as she returned home with a full water jar, she gave birth to Rinpoche without injury. His mother's name was Sönam Lhamo. His father was a natural yogin called Ge Tamdrin. Rinpoche's mother later told him, "Your birth caused me no difficulty."

We Tibetans have a long-standing tradition of appraising the auspiciousness or virtue of an event by the signs that accompany it. Among such signs, those accompanying Rinpoche's birth are extraordinarily good, heralding his long and extraordinary life. The

31. Dharmapalas are deities who protect Buddhism and those who practice it.

occurrence of his birth while his mother was carrying
a full water jar, at sunrise, and on a sacred day are all
extremely auspicious. These signs have both dharmic
and worldly implications. If we apply them to dharma,
the full water jar was a sign that this holy being's mind
would be filled with compassion and bodhichitta.
However one cannot traverse the paths and stages,
and help beings, through means alone. The glorious
Chandrakirti wrote:

> With spread white wings of relative and absolute
>   truth
> The king of swans leads ordinary swans onward.
> Riding the winds of virtue they reach
> The far shore of the ocean of the victors' qualities.

As he wrote, both means and wisdom are necessary.
The occurrence of Rinpoche's birth at sunrise was a
sign of his primordial awareness, his wisdom. His
birth on a day sacred to the dharmapalas was a sign of
his strength and power. Therefore the signs at
Rinpoche's birth indicated that with the power of
means and wisdom, he would accomplish perfect
transcendence for his own good, perfect realization
for others' good, and perfect benefit of beings for the
good of both himself and others.

> Because you'd gathered the two accumulations
>   over many kalpas,[32]

32. The two accumulations are the accumulation of merit and of wisdom.

As soon as your marks of a protector of beings
   were revealed,
Millions of auspicious signs of virtue blazed
   with glory.
The signs of a holy being were spontaneously
   present.

Rock with Amitayus sutra and stupa carved by Rinpoche's father. Rinpoche's younger sister, Tsekyi Tsomo, and younger brother, Karma Yeshe, stand on the carved rock releasing prayer flags. Margori in the eastern part of Rapshul Nyengyal, East Tibet, 2006.

Chapter Three
The Greatness of His Parents and Family

The author's parents, Rinpoche's younger brother and his wife, Kham, East Tibet, 2004.

The Greatness of His Parents and Family

It is said that Rinpoche's ancestors were oracles. However I do not know much about them and therefore cannot tell you more than that.

Rinpoche's father, while around twenty, carved the *Amitayus Sutra* and a stupa on a flat rock stuck into the side of a mountain called Margori in the eastern part of Rapshul Nyengyal. He afterward invited the master from Thrangu Monastery, Koru Karma Dargyay, to consecrate and view the carvings.[33] The master said, "As you have carved the *Amitayus Sutra* in a location with excellent geomancy, you are definitely going to have a lot of children and many of them are going to be amazing." As predicted, Rinpoche's parents had ten children: six sons and four daughters. Rinpoche was the fourth child.

Rinpoche's father's root guru was a teacher of the

33. *Author's note:* As clearly described in my book *Kham Masters.*

34. *Author's note:*
As clearly
described in my
book Kham
Masters.

great perfection called Drimay Özer the Yogin.[34] On
sacred days, Rinpoche's father always practiced
Embodiment of the Three Jewels. He had an old set of
cymbals, and Rinpoche said that when his father
played them during the invitation of Guru Rinpoche,
Rinpoche always felt, even at the age of five, that the
deity had actually arrived. Unable to stand the inten-
sity of his faith and delight, Rinpoche would run out
of the room, cry, and even dance.

Rinpoche's father chanted both *Self-Liberated*
Aggregates: The Liberation Through Wearing of the
Peaceful and Wrathful Ones and *Recitation of*
Manjushri's Names every day. Especially he chanted
Recitation of Manjushri's Names many times each day.
At night when he went to sleep, he would stop chant-
ing *Recitation of Manjushri's Names* at whatever point
he had reached in it. When he awoke the next morn-
ing, he would resume chanting from exactly where he
had left off the night before.

Rinpoche's father was an honest and forthright person, but he was also inexorable if the situation was
important. There are many stories about this, but the
following will serve as an example.

He kept his herd of livestock in a place called
Nyengyal Betri Guntser, where the pastures were
shared by four neighbors. Above the pastures was a
mountain of rock. One day after the animals were
herded into their corral, seven bandits started shoot-
ing at them from behind rocks on the mountainside.

Terrified, the animals broke their tethers, burst out of the corral, and started to run off in all directions. One of the neighbors, a fainthearted man named Dargyay, shot back at the bandits from the corral, but allowed the livestock to escape. Once the animals were out of the corral, the bandits raced their horses and started to herd the animals away. Although they tried to keep the herds divided, in all the confusion they became mixed together. So the bandits rode off as a group, driving all the herds along as one mass.

Rinpoche's father came running up, holding a spear. Dargyay and a few others brought Rinpoche's father his unsaddled horse. Rinpoche's father said to Dargyay, "Those bandits are still close. Grab your rifle and we'll chase them!"

Dargyay was afraid, and answered, "My gun's jammed; it won't fire!" Immediately Rinpoche's father mounted his unsaddled horse and, gripping his spear, chased after the bandits. When he got close, the bandits saw him. Yelling eagerly about who was going to shoot their pursuer, the bandits set two horn rifle-braces on a hearthstone.[35] Rinpoche's father continued to ride straight at them. One after another, the bandits shot five bullets at him, but neither he nor his horse was hit. Rinpoche's father jumped his horse right over the hearthstone and into the midst of the bandits. In their surprise, the bandits scattered. Dargyay showed up then and shot twice in the direction of the fleeing bandits, proving that his gun had

35. Tibetan rifle braces were often made of horn.

not jammed. The bandits returned home with empty hands and bowed heads. Not one of the animals was lost; they were all recovered.

Drimay Özer the Yogin taught the ejection of consciousness to both of Rinpoche's parents and his grandmother. All three of them demonstrated the signs of ejection through the aperture of Brahma.

Rinpoche tells the story that in 1960 his brother, Khenpo Södo, who had been living in the upper room of Zuru Rinpoche's residence, was no longer there.[36] In order to guard the residence, Rinpoche's father slept there every night. A monk named Pawo and his sister, a nun named Rikdzin Drölma, lived downstairs.

One night Rinpoche's father said to them, "Although I'm not at all ill, I feel dizzy and unsteady on my feet. Tonight I'm going to sleep downstairs."

That night he lay down in their room. They talked late into the night, until finally Rinpoche's father seemed unable to speak clearly. He said, "I am very happy." Then he became quiet. Well into the night they heard him exclaim "PHAT" several times. When the sun shone into Zuru Rinpoche's residence the next morning, Rinpoche's father was dead. It is certain that he had performed the ejection of consciousness that night.

In the same year, Rinpoche's grandmother passed away. She died with her palms joined in prayer.

Rinpoche's mother was an extremely kind person

36. The Zuru Rinpoches are one of the incarnation lines of Thrangu Monastery.

with a great deal of compassion. Every year Drimay
Özer the Yogin held a hundred nyungnays.[37] One year
Rinpoche's mother attended this and performed all
hundred. While doing so, she took care of three blind
elderly men who were also present.

Rinpoche's eldest brother was Khenpo Karma
Tsewang. He studied at the college of Thrangu
Monastery under the guidance of Khenpo Ngedön.
Then he went to Tserey Monastery where he continued to study for another three years under the
guidance of Tserey Khenpo. After that, he returned
to Thrangu Monastery, where he served for eleven
years as both khenpo and vajracharya.[38] He also
performed a three-year retreat in the six dharmas
of Naropa retreat facility. When Khenpo Lodrö
Rapsal of Shechen became the khenpo of Thrangu
Monastery's college, Karma Tsewang remained at
the college for five more years. Then he vowed to
remain in retreat for another three years in a
retreat building called the Red Retreat.[39] Toward
the end of the three years, Thrangu Monastery was
destroyed during the Communist invasion. Karma
Tsewang made no attempt to escape and was captured by the invading army.

As Karma Tsewang had a fair face with red cheeks,
he acquired the nickname *Gyayung Mari*, which
means "Turnip Red-Spots." From then on, he and
his brothers were called the "Gyayung family" for
that reason.

37. A nyungnay is
a two-day fasting
and Avalokita
meditation retreat.

38. A khenpo is
both a preceptor
and a professor of
Buddhist scholar-
ship. A vajracharya
is a master of
tantric ritual and
meditation.

39. *Author's note:*
This building was
called the Red
Retreat because
one of the previous
Shamar Rinpoches
had done a retreat
there.

Translator's note:
Shamar means
"Red Crown."

Rinpoche's brother, Lama Sönam, outside his retreat at Takmo Lujin, Nepal, 2004.

Rinpoche's sister, Pema Lhakyi, bearing a gift for Rinpoche at his birthday celebration, Karma Triyana Dharmachakra, 2004.

Karma Tsewang wrote the following stanza:

> I take refuge in the guru and the three jewels.
> I pray to the guru and the three jewels.
> May my parents, all beings, never be separated
>   from the guru
> Or the three jewels in this life, future lives, or the
>   bardo.

Rinpoche's other elder brother was Lama Södo. It was planned that he would remain in the retreat at Thrangu Monastery for twelve years and then serve as its retreat master. However after eleven years in retreat, he was captured by the invading army. He had drawn his winds into his avadhuti, as is evidenced by the fact that he could perform many yogic exercises within a single breath.[40]

40. The avadhuti is the central channel of the body.

One of Rinpoche's younger brothers is Lama Sönam, who performed two three-year retreats in the six dharmas of Naropa retreat facility at Takmo Lujin, a sacred place in Nepal. Since then he has remained as a lifelong retreatant and has completed a hundred million recitations of the mantra OM MANI PADME HUM.

Another of Rinpoche's younger brothers is my father, Karma Yeshe. He has great faith in the dharma of all traditions, and recites daily the *Recitation of Manjushri's Names*, the *Amitayus Sutra*, and prayers to Guru Rinpoche including the *Seven Chapters*, *Removing Obstacles from the Path*, and *Spontaneous Fulfillment of Wishes*. Every morning he performs a hundred prostrations while chanting Karma Chakme's *Sukhavati Aspiration*. In the evening he and his entire family chant the praises of White and Green Tara three times each, as well as *Removing Obstacles from the Path*, and *Spontaneous Fulfillment of Wishes*. He is stalwart in friendship and enmity, and is also forthright. Because he is attentive to the results of actions, he is greatly respected in his area. Although one could easily criticize me for writing in praise of my own father, the Buddha permitted telling the truth.

Rinpoche's youngest brother and an older sister are deceased.

His sister Pema Lhakyi has recited the mantra OM MANI PADME HUM two hundred million times and now lives in Shijam, China.

Rinpoche's younger sister, Tsekyi Tsomo, is the mother of Lodrö Nyima Tulku Rinpoche and has immeasurable faith in dharma. Rinpoche's youngest sister, Tashi Wangmo, also has great natural faith in dharma.

Rinpoche, our kind guru, loved to fight as a child and was implacable. Once he got into a fight with Kojo Gyalsay Tulku, a young lama from Ranyak Monastery who was several years older than Rinpoche. Rinpoche barely reached the tulku's shoulders, and eventually the tulku was able to throw Rinpoche to the ground. Rinpoche's head landed on a horn stake, causing him to bleed. When the tulku saw that Rinpoche was bleeding, he became afraid of what

Rinpoche's mother would say and tried to stop the flow of blood. Rinpoche's mother arrived and staunched the bleeding with dough and bandaged the wound. The tulku said, "I have blessed you so that from now on you will never suffer a head wound."

On one occasion after that incident Rinpoche accidentally struck his head against a wall. His head landed against a small stone protrusion. This damaged his skull, and even now the bone in that part of his head is still slightly uneven. However there was no external skin wound.

On another occasion Rinpoche and his brother Karma Tsewang were running in play in the pastures. Rinpoche ran so quickly that when he found himself at the edge of a rock cliff the height of a single story, he was unable to stop and fell off the cliff. When he landed he struck his head against a flat rock with such force that the sound echoed and Rinpoche became unconscious. The only damage he suffered was a temporary swollen bruise on his head; there was no bleeding. Rinpoche said that the tulku must have really blessed him.

Rinpoche was very fond of bows, arrows, knives, and other weapons. He was an excellent archer as well as skilled in the making of bows, arrows, and anything made of wood. Because Rinpoche often playfully mimicked violent behavior, such as stabbing people with a knife, his father worried that if Rinpoche did not become a monk he would bring himself great danger.

One night while he was a child, Rinpoche dreamed that he went to a land that he had never seen before. There were many tall buildings, the people were wearing unfamiliar clothing, and there were many different types of automobiles. Rinpoche said that when he later arrived in New York City in the United States, things were just as in his dream.

Rinpoche's father taught him how to read and write proficiently. While he lived with his parents, Rinpoche herded livestock and sheep. He said that often, when he had to search for a lost animal, he ended up sleeping in the wilderness.

Rinpoche sometimes carved the mantra OM MANI PADME HUM in stone. It is said that in Chumar and other places Rinpoche carved the six syllables, with large letters, into the rock with great skill.

One day Rinpoche and his father went to the Old Cave at Nyengyal and carved the MANI into the rocks, having received sponsorship for this over the previous month. On the way back home, Rinpoche's father led him to the place where he had carved the *Amitayus Sutra*. As it had become covered by grass, they cleared this away and set stones around it to keep it clear. Rinpoche says that his father treasured that *Amitayus Sutra*.

Through your good aspirations you were born in a
   good family.
You repaid your parents' kindness in many ways.
You had even then the ability to learn so many
   things.
In signs and dreams you saw the future.

Chapter Four

The Greatness of His Renunciation of Home Life for the Victor's Teachings and His Dharma Training in the Monastery

Vairochana retreat house, Thrangu Monastery, Kham, East Tibet, 2006.

The Greatness of His Renunciation of Home Life for the Victor's Teachings and His Dharma Training in the Monastery

When Rinpoche was twelve he renounced home life and became a monastic at Tashi Chöling in western Ga, also known as Thrangu Monastery. His master at the time was Khenpo Ngedön, although from time to time Khenpo Ngedön was unable to control him. Rinpoche memorized the liturgy of the monastery and fulfilled his other responsibilities there.

When Rinpoche was fifteen the Sixteenth Gyalwang Karmapa, with a retinue of more than a hundred, came to Thrangu Monastery and stayed there for about a month. Every day the Karmapa bestowed two public empowerments and displayed the Great Black Crown that Liberates upon Sight. Rinpoche had the good fortune to attend all of these events. In those days it was customary that a hundredfold offering be made on each occasion that the Black

Crown was displayed. Most of the donors in the area received an opportunity to do this during the course of that month. Rinpoche's parents also visited the monastery during that month in order to receive empowerment and see the Black Crown.

When Rinpoche was sixteen, as was customary at Thrangu Monastery, he went on pilgrimage to Lhasa in the company of other monks. They traveled on foot, carrying their provisions on their backs. The journey there and back took six months. That year Rinpoche celebrated Losar in Lhasa. At Tsurphu Monastery he again met the Sixteenth Gyalwang Karmapa, who was by that time seventeen.[41] Rinpoche drank from the Shongpa Lhachu and saw the Jowo of Lhasa.[42]

As the Karmapa was seventeen at the time, it was not yet time for him to bestow the vows of shramanera or bhikshu.[43] Therefore Rinpoche went to Palpung Monastery at the age of twenty and received the bhikshu vows from Situ Pema Wangchok Gyalpo, who bestowed upon him the name Karma Sönam Gyurmay.[44]

You saw sacred places and the Black Crown that
    Liberates upon Sight.
Your past aspirations and virtuous habits were
    awakened.
You properly received the precious moral
    discipline pleasing to the victors
And are magnificent amidst the saffron-adorned.[45]

41. Author's note: The Sixteenth Gyalwang Karmapa and Khenpo Rinpoche were born in the same year.

42. The Shongpa Lhachu is a spring believed to be of miraculous origin. The Jowo is a famous image of the Buddha in Lhasa; it is regarded as the most sacred image in all of Tibet.

43. A shramanera is a novice monk; a bhikshu is a full monk.

44. This name means "unchanging merit."

45. "Saffron-adorned" refers to Buddhist monastics.

Chapter Five
The Greatness of His Learning, Reflection, and Meditation

The Second Jamgön Rinpoche, Palden Khyentse Özer (1902-1953), Tsadra Rinchen Drak, Derge, Kham, Tibet, mid 1940s. With the Chinese destruction, this photograph was buried in the rest of the rubble. Many years later, it was found undamaged. The present Jamgön Rinpoche's secretary, Tendzin Dorje, brought the picture to the United States to make copies. He gave the original to Khenpo Karthar Rinpoche, which Rinpoche has in his room and from which this photograph was taken.

The Greatness of His Learning, Reflection, and Meditation

That same year, after returning to Thrangu Monastery, Rinpoche entered the Vairochana retreat and remained there for one year.[46] He then did a three-year retreat in the six dharmas of Naropa retreat of Thrangu Monastery under the guidance of the retreat master Karma Sherab, a disciple of Karma Tsultrim. Rinpoche said that during those three years he did not even once quarrel with either his retreat master or his fellow retreatants.

The Second Jamgön Rinpoche, Palden Khyentse Özer, visited the retreat and bestowed numerous empowerments and transmissions such as the transmission of and instruction on the "Short Vajradhara" lineage supplication. Rinpoche received all of these.

After completing the three-year-three-phase

46. Vairochana is an important meditation deity in both Tibetan and Japanese Buddhism.

retreat, Rinpoche donned a single cotton robe and circumambulated the monastery three times. He did not feel cold in spite of the fact that it was an extremely cold day. When the freezing wind hit him, Rinpoche experienced it as refreshing, like a cool breeze on a hot summer day. Rinpoche said that his experience of warmth and bliss at that time arose through the force of blessing.[47]

47. It is customary for those who complete a retreat on the six dharmas of Naropa to demonstrate their control over body temperature by publicly donning thin cotton robes on a cold winter day and forming a procession, enabling spectators to see who shivers and who does not.

As one of the monks in the Vairochana retreat had died, Rinpoche took his place for six months. Then Jamgön Palden Khyentse Özer returned to Thrangu Monastery. While addressing the community he said, "If you can recite a hundred million MANI mantras in this life, I guarantee that you will be freed from lower rebirths!"

As our kind, great guru had already planned on doing this, Jamgön Rinpoche's words spurred him to a decision. He decided to spend the rest of his life in retreat. He sold all his belongings except a few articles of clothing in order to gather provisions for retreat. He remained for a few months in the Red Retreat, the practice place of his uncle, Ge Karma Sabchu.

48. Traleg Kyabgön Rinpoche is one of the foremost incarnate teachers from Thrangu Monastery. Shechen Jamgön Rinpoche was one of five contemporary emanations of Jamgön Kongtrul the Great.

When Rinpoche was twenty-six, Traleg Rinpoche said to him insistently, "As Shechen Kongtrul Rinpoche has come here, it would be more beneficial to beings and the teachings for you to enter the college than to remain alone in retreat for your whole life. You must leave your retreat!" So Rinpoche left his retreat in obedience to that insistent command.[48]

Kyapjay Thrangu Rinpoche, Karma Dongak, the lifelong retreatant Tsoknyi, and Rinpoche received the transmission of the *Treasury of Knowledge* from Shechen Kongtrul Rinpoche.[49] Then Shechen Khenpo Lodrö Rapsal became the khenpo of the Thrangu college. Along with his brother Khenpo Karma Tsewang, Karma Damchö, Thrangu Rinpoche (who was fourteen when he entered the college), and others, Rinpoche studied at the college of Thrangu Monastery for five years. Khenpo Lodrö Rapsal taught them the *Bodhicharyavatara*, the *Abhidharmakosha*, the *Madhyamakavatara*, the *Abhisamayalankara*, the *Uttaratantra*, the *Madhyantavibhanga*, and the *Dharmadharmatavibhanga*, all according to the commentaries by Mipham.

During this time a skilled seer came to Thrangu Monastery and remained there for a few days. The monks each asked about their futures. The seer accurately predicted what would happen to each of them. When our kind guru asked about his future he was told, "You will plant a yellow prayer flag on the peak of a high mountain. It will be blown back and forth by the wind, but I don't know why." Rinpoche said this seems to have been a prediction of his having to serve both Thrangu Monastery and Karma Triyana Dharmachakra after going to America.

When Rinpoche was thirty-one, the Sixteenth Gyalwang Karmapa visited Palpung Monastery. Rinpoche went to meet him again and received

49. The *Treasury of Knowledge* is one of the *Five Treasuries* of Jamgön Kongtrul the Great.

numerous empowerments and transmissions. From the age of thirty-one until he was thirty-six, Rinpoche traveled with Kyapjay Thrangu Rinpoche through the nomad country, performing ceremonies at the request of various patrons. Khenpo Rinpoche was also appointed the manager of Thrangu Rinpoche's residence.

Khenpo Gangshar visited Thrangu Monastery for two days and presented guidance on the mind to more than five hundred monks. Khenpo Karthar Rinpoche said that as soon as he saw Khenpo Gangshar, he felt unfabricated devotion for him as a mahasiddha like Tilopa or Naropa.[50]

50. Khenpo Gangshar was a renowned teacher of mahamudra and dzokchen.

In the year 1958, because of the changing times, Rinpoche fled the region along with Kyapjay Thrangu Rinpoche, Traleg Rinpoche, Zuru Tulku, Khenpo Rinpoche's younger brother Lama Sönam Chodar, and several monks. Before they left, Rinpoche insistently asked his eldest brother Khenpo Karma Tsewang, who was living in the Red Retreat; and his elder brother Sönam Dorje, who was in the three-year retreat facility, to flee along with the others. Both of them gave him the same answer: "You must serve the Rinpoches by getting them to safety. As we are in retreat, we will remain here and await whatever comes. We will not leave retreat in such haste." There was nothing Rinpoche could do to change their minds.

Around this time Rinpoche dreamed that he was

Vajrayogini, with a body the size of a mountain, float-ing above the clouds.[51] Looking down, he saw that a fierce hailstorm was falling on all the mountains and valleys. They were also being devastated by thunder and lightning. Rinpoche, up in the sky, was unharmed. He recognized this to be a sign that he would reach safety, and so he left, beginning his long journey to India.

One of those with Rinpoche was a tutor from Thrangu Monastery named Chöden. The Thrangu Upasaka appeared to Chöden in a dream and told him, "I have to go to China. You lamas and monks must reach India."[52] The Upasaka then purified Chöden with water from a vase. As predicted in that dream, they were able to reach India without great difficulty.

Fifteen days into their journey, they were detected and fired upon by the invading army. During the attack, Rinpoche imagined that he carried the Gyalwang Karmapa on his back like a shield and prayed with fervor as he ran. He was not shot. After two and a half months, they all arrived at Tsurphu. The Sixteenth Gyalwang Karmapa kindly met with the lamas and monks from Thrangu Monastery. While speaking to them, he glanced at our kind guru and said jokingly, "Although we usually need to imagine our guru above our head, there are some people who imagine their guru on their back like a cloak!" Then he laughed.

51. Vajrayogini is one of the three principal yidams of the Karma Kagyu tradition.

52. An upasaka is a Buddhist with nonmonastic pratimoksha vows. The Thrangu Upasaka is a nonhuman being who holds such vows and actively aids and supports Thrangu Monastery.

His Holiness the Sixteenth Karmapa, Rangjung Rigpe Dorje, 1923-1981, with the Eleventh Tai Situ Rinpoche, Pema Wangchok Gyalpo, 1886-1952, Tibet, 1940s.

Knowing that the Gyalwang Karmapa had seen him with his eyes of unobscured wisdom, Rinpoche wept.

The blessing of a realized guru will suddenly enter
A person with devotion and faith.
That is why the peerless Dakpo Kagyu
Is also called the Lineage of Devotion.

Then, as commanded by the Gyalwang Karmapa, they resumed their journey, leaving Tsurphu on March 7th, 1959. They loaded their possessions onto five yaks. The three tulkus rode on horseback. All the others walked on foot, which made the journey exhausting. In two weeks they reached the border of Tibet and Bhutan. As they were not immediately permitted to enter Bhutan, they had to remain at the border for about a month.

Eventually Rinpoche arrived in the refugee camp in Buxa, India. During the nine years he spent there, he studied with lamas and monks of all traditions in order to best serve the Buddha's teachings. From the prayer for Rinpoche's longevity composed by the Seventeenth Gyalwang Karmapa:

The good vase of your heart is filled with the
    amrita of scripture and reason.

Rinpoche became slightly ill while living in Buxa because of the heat. One night he dreamed that he found himself amidst an encampment of demons.

Suddenly a shaggy, fat, white lamb appeared. Rinpoche jumped onto its back. Riding the lamb and driving off the demons by hitting them with a rope he was holding, he escaped. While a child, our kind guru often dreamed of a handsome little boy who could cleverly respond to anything said to him. Based on the demeanor of the boy, Rinpoche could predict the successful or unsuccessful outcome of anything he did. Once he reached India, the boy became a lamb. Rinpoche said both the boy and the lamb were images of his spirit.[53]

One night Rinpoche dreamed that a headless dog attacked him. He rolled the dog up into a ball and threw it outside. When the dog returned and again attacked him, Rinpoche felt great compassion and said to it, "Consume my flesh and blood as you wish." The dog was unable to harm him, however, and disappeared. Nevertheless two monks from Thrangu Monastery and one monk from Benchen Monastery who lived with Rinpoche died. Rinpoche said that it seems that Buxa is haunted by the ghosts of many Indians whom the British forces executed there and also by the ghosts of British soldiers who died there.

After that, Rinpoche recovered from his illness and went on pilgrimage all over India with his brother Lama Sönam and others. Traveling by train, Rinpoche and his brother became separated from their companions in the crowd of passengers and ended up at the wrong destination. They were stuck there for two days

53. The word *spirit* here is a translation of the Tibetan *bla* (pronounced "la"), which refers to a component of a person that is believed to protect them during life and remain with their body after death.

without any food. My uncle, Lama Sönam Chödar, says, "Even though we had not eaten for two days, Karthar could still walk fast and didn't seem hungry. I could hardly see from hunger and couldn't walk straight!"

In 1967 Rinpoche went to Rumtek Monastery. For more than a year he taught the monks there and also performed ceremonies for the lay community. Then, at the command of the Gyalwang Karmapa, Rinpoche went to Tilokpur Nunnery. He remained there for a year and a half, teaching the *Bodhicharyavatara* and other dharma to about thirty nuns. Then he returned to Rumtek.

The Gyalwang Karmapa next sent Rinpoche to Dungkar Tashi Chöling, a monastery in Bhutan sponsored by the Bhutanese government. Rinpoche was sent there to be the abbot in charge of the rainy season retreat. At the time our kind guru remarked jokingly to Bayö Rinpoche, "I know nothing about presiding over rainy season retreats. Since the Gyalwang Karmapa is sending me to do so, perhaps through his compassion it will come to me in a vision!" Bayö Rinpoche said that when he repeated this conversation to the Gyalwang Karmapa, the Karmapa laughed a lot.

After that rainy season retreat, the Gyalwang Karmapa bestowed the monastery of Tashi Chöling in eastern Bhutan on the monks from Thrangu

Monastery. The elderly lama from the protector temple, Lama Karma Tashi, Lama Chöden, Lama Sönam, and Rinpoche remained there for one year.

Rinpoche then went to Khamtrul Rinpoche's monastery in Bhutan, Tashi Jong. For four months he received from Dilgo Khyentse Rinpoche all of the empowerments and transmissions of the *Treasury of Instructions*.[54]

Lama Chöden had been serving as the manager of all the monks from Thrangu Monastery who had reached India. After he passed away, the Thrangu Upasaka appeared to our kind guru in a dream and told him, "Now that the manager has passed away, there is no one more qualified than you to replace him. You must do so!" Then the Upasaka disappeared.

When Rinpoche awoke, he worriedly thought, "How could I possibly replace the late manager?" However so many monks had died that there was no one else to accept the responsibility.

Years later, when the Gyalwang Karmapa sent Rinpoche to the United States, he experienced no difficulty during his journey, and after settling in America was able to further serve Thrangu Monastery. Rinpoche says that both of these were due to the kindness of the Gyalwang Karmapa and the assistance of the Thrangu Upasaka.

While fulfilling all the responsibilities given him by the Gyalwang Karmapa, Rinpoche suffered from

54. The *Treasury of Instructions* is one of the *Five Treasuries*.

tuberculosis for five years. Finally his condition became so severe that he was admitted to the hospital and remained there for eleven months. During that time, he was given more food and medicine than other patients. He gave half of what he received to others, and also tried to assist the other patients in every way he could. He became respected and loved by everyone in the hospital. Rinpoche says that the medicine offered to him by his disciples in America is the result of his generosity in the Indian hospital.

Rinpoche became so ill that he was close to death. One night he dreamed that he was climbing up a very narrow path on an extremely steep mountain. In front of him was the lamb he had dreamed of before, but it was now yellow instead of white, and it was covered in dirt. The lamb was so weak that Rinpoche had to help support it. Rinpoche himself was supported by two uncles of the Gyalwang Karmapa: Gönpo Namgyal on his right, and Rinchen Namgyal on his left. Together they climbed until the path began to widen. Finally Rinpoche no longer needed their help and flew off by himself. He landed on top of a small mountain. He dreamed then of various places and people, some of them clear and some unclear. Rinpoche says that they were like the present site, the surrounding area, and the people of Karma Triyana Dharmachakra; and that the dream also indicated that the Gyalwang Karmapa saved his life.

Adorned by the qualities of learning, reflection,
and meditation,
You battled the thousand dangers of war's foul
windstorm
And escorted great beings to safety
In India, the land of dharma.

With the Sixteenth Karmapa, from a video taken at a gallery in New York, ca. 1976.

Chapter Six
The Greatness of His Title and Place of Residence

Khenpo Karthar Rinpoche when he first arrived in the
United States, New York, 1976.

The Greatness of His Title
and Place of Residence

Then the Gyalwang Karmapa sent his attendant Tsewang Paljor to Bhutan to summon Rinpoche to Rumtek. When Rinpoche arrived in Rumtek as commanded, the Gyalwang Karmapa said to him, "You must go now to New York, in the United States of America."

For the sake of auspiciousness, the Gyalwang Karmapa and his monks gathered in the temple to recite prayers of aspiration, and all who were assembled there were offered rice and tea. The Gyalwang Karmapa presented both Lama Gendun from Kyodrak Monastery and Khenpo Rinpoche with scarves and the title "Lord of Dharma."[55]

In March of 1976 Lama Gendun, with one monk to assist him; Mr. Tendzin Chönyi, with Yeshe Namdak

55. A number of lamas are referred to in this sixth chapter. Lama Gendun, who is no longer alive, was a great master from Kyodrak Monastery. He became the resident teacher (continued)

55. (continued)

at Dakpo Kagyu Ling in France. Mr. Tendzin Chönyi is the president of Karma Triyana Dharmachakra, the Gyalwang Karmapa's seat in North America. Yeshe Namdak of Rumtek Monastery lived and worked for many years at Karma Triyana Dharmachakra and is now deceased. Lama Ganga, also deceased, was a renowned meditation master from Thrangu Monastery. Trungpa Rinpoche, originally from Surmang Monastery, was a Karma Kagyu master whose teachings and activity in North America have been so influential that he is, twenty years after his passing, legendary. Jamgön Rinpoche was the Third Jamgön Kongtrul Rinpoche of Palpung Monastery. He passed away in 1992 and has since been reborn and recognized by the Gyalwang Karmapa. Lama Norlha of Goche Monastery is the spiritual director of Kagyu Thubten Chöling in Wappingers Falls, New York and its affiliates throughout the eastern United States. Bardor Tulku Rinpoche is a reincarnation of the great treasure-revealer Barway Dorje. He teaches both at Karma Triyana Dharmachakra and at his own center, Kunzang Palchen Ling, in Red Hook, New York.

Bardor Tulku Rinpoche, Khenpo Karthar Rinpoche, Lama Ganga, and Lama Norlha, old shrine room, Karma Triyana Dharmachakra, 1980.

as his assistant; and Khenpo Rinpoche, with Lama Ganga as his assistant were sent to New York City in the eastern United States.

In 1977 both the Gyalwang Karmapa and Trungpa Rinpoche visited New York. During their visit, our kind guru Khenpo Rinpoche gave his first dharma teaching to Americans. In a large hotel in New York City, Rinpoche spoke to a public audience of more than a thousand about the great qualities of the Gyalwang Karmapa. The Karmapa, who was pleased by the talk, said jokingly to Rinpoche, "I had no idea you could talk so much, so cleverly, or with such style!" After the talk, the Gyalwang Karmapa kindly publicly displayed the Great Black Crown that Liberates upon Sight.

At that time the khenpos and tulkus in the Gyalwang Karmapa's party were staying outside New York City in Putnam County, where the Taiwanese donor Dr. Shen offered the Gyalwang Karmapa three hundred acres of land. The Karmapa named the land Norbuling. One day the Gyalwang Karmapa and our kind guru went for a walk around the land. While they were walking, the Karmapa said, "Although I named this place Norbuling, we must call it Norbugang. Also, the dharma center here must hold its opening ceremony on the fifteenth day of the month Vaishakha next year."[56] Rinpoche replied, "Yes, of course", but he did not know what the Karmapa was thinking. It later turned out that there

56. *Norbuling* means "Jewel Park." *Norbugang* means "Jewel Ridge." The fifteenth day of the month Vaishakha is the day on which the Buddha is believed to have achieved awakening.

was a small public thoroughfare crossing the property, and nothing could be built on it.

Then Jamgön Rinpoche and Lama Norlha found the property on which our monastery was eventually built.[57] The tulkus and khenpos visited the property, and a price was immediately agreed upon. The opening ceremony of the new center was held, just as the Gyalwang Karmapa had foreseen with his eyes of unobscured wisdom, on the fifteenth day of the month Vaishakha. The Karmapa named the monastery Karma Triyana Dharmachakra.[58] When he was later asked to name the centers affiliated with the monastery, the Gyalwang Karmapa replied, "You can call the affiliated centers whatever you want. You don't need to always ask me!"

At that time our kind guru said to the Gyalwang Karmapa and the donors there, "Thank you for enabling me to come to America. My health has improved!"

The Karmapa replied, "If you were still in India now, you would be close to death."

In 1980 the Gyalwang Karmapa returned to the United States. Although the monastery's shrine building had not yet been built, there was a fairly large old house on the property. There the Karmapa kindly bestowed teachings, empowerments, and transmissions. He told our kind guru that year, "If you had remained in Rumtek, you would be dead now."

During that visit, the Gyalwang Karmapa went to

57. This property and the monastery built there are in Woodstock, New York.

58. The monastery's name means "Karmapa's Dharma Wheel of the Three Vehicles." The three vehicles are the common vehicle, the great vehicle or mahayana, and the vajra vehicle or vajrayana.

Rinpoche's birthday celebration, Karma Triyana
Dharmachakra, ca. 1995.

New York City. While he was there, it became necessary to dig a well for the monastery. It was a hot summer, and water was scarce. The well was dug to a depth of five hundred feet, but no water appeared. Tendzinla called the Karmapa on the telephone.[59] The Gyalwang Karmapa told him that Bardor Tulku Rinpoche and the other lamas should offer a golden drink.[60] The Karmapa said that he saw a regional god of America, golden in color, covering the water table under the ground with his hand and preventing the well from accessing the water. The Gyalwang Karmapa then dictated to Jamgön Rinpoche a liturgy compelling the golden guardian of the earth to assist and not obstruct his activity. This liturgy is still in daily use at Karma Triyana Dharmachakra.

When Bardor Rinpoche and the others offered the golden drink, water appeared. The Karmapa said that the golden guardian of the earth is a great protector of the United States of America.

During that summer, whenever Khenpo Rinpoche started to do any manual labor, the Gyalwang Karmapa said to him, "I have sent you here as my representative and given you the title Lord of Dharma. Sit down. You don't need to do any physical work."

In the fall of 1981, in Zion, Illinois, the Gyalwang Karmapa passed into the dharmadhatu for the good of disciples in other realms.[61] Khenpo Rinpoche visited him before he passed away, and Rinpoche began to weep from grief. The Karmapa said to him, "Don't

59. Tendzinla is Mr. Tendzin Chönyi. The suffix "la" connotes respect.

60. A golden drink is a libation offering containing powdered gold and jewels.

61. When awakened beings pass away, they are said to pass into the dharmadhatu. The dharmadhatu is the natural expanse, the nature of everything.

worry! I'm leaving my body here, but my mind will go to Tibet. I have a lot of people here to take care of me; you don't need to stay. Do your best to console and teach the disciples in our dharma centers. That will fulfill my wishes."

For the next six months our kind guru taught and encouraged disciples in our affiliate centers, both those centers that already existed and those he founded then. He was assisted by two interpreters: Ngödrup Tsering Burkhar and Chökyong Radha.[62] Rinpoche says that during that time he and his two interpreters would often break into tears in the middle of talks because of their grief at the Gyalwang Karmapa's passing.

At that time most of the disciples were thinking, "The Gyalwang Karmapa has passed away! What are we going to do?" They were very discouraged. Khenpo Rinpoche's main advice to them was that the Karmapa's rebirth would soon appear, and until then his disciples needed to strengthen their dharma practice and increase the activity of their centers. His advice helped a great deal.

On one of his visits to New York City, the Gyalwang Karmapa had blood drawn for various tests. He kept three vials of his blood, and wrapped them up in a kata to which he affixed his seal. He gave the vials of his blood to Khenpo Rinpoche and said to him, "Agama, keep these."[63]

After the Karmapa's passing, Rinpoche thought,

62. Ngödrup Burkhar is a well-known Tibetan interpreter who has translated not only for Khenpo Karthar Rinpoche but also for both the Sixteenth and Seventeenth Gyalwang Karmapas and many other masters. Chökyong Radha, who passed away on August 30th, 2008, was Khenpo Karthar Rinpoche's primary interpreter for many years.

63. *Agama* is an East Tibetan term of endearment, usually used when speaking to family members or close friends.

"Although the Gyalwang Karmapa has passed away, his rebirth will soon appear. Until then, I must make pills out of his blood for the benefit of others!" Rinpoche made many of these pills and gave them to the mortally ill and others. He continues even now to benefit many beings by giving them these pills.

The Gyalwang Karmapa had founded more than forty centers in the United States and other countries that were under Khenpo Rinpoche's supervision. In those centers there was a great deal of practice going on, including the Avalokita, Amitabha, and nyungnay practices; and the meditation practices of tranquility and insight. Rinpoche says that at first and for several years, he taught only tranquility meditation. As disciples began to mature, he started to bestow empowerments and deepen his instructions.

The Karmapa, the bearer of the Black Crown,
Blessed you with his three secrets.
He declared you a Lord of Dharma, a scion of
    the victors.
In one instant, your wisdom-awareness display
    was complete.

Khenpo Rinpoche with a traditional Tibetan wood-block text,
New York Karma Thegsum Chöling, ca. 1984.

Chapter Seven
The Greatness of His Skill in All Crafts

Rinpoche at work, artist's studio, Woodstock, New York, early 1980s.

The Greatness of His Skill in All Crafts

Wherever our kind guru lives, he works harder than anyone else. He makes and sews the decorative banners and victory banners for our shrine rooms, the brocade frames for paintings, and robes for monastics. He makes dharani rolls and fills statues with them.[64] He creates the decorations for stupas and statues, using pearls and gems. He paints and gilds statues. He is an expert in geomancy, the making of tormas, and judging the quality of gold, silver, turquoise, coral, and amber. He is a brilliant teacher of sutra and tantra, and especially of mahamudra. His knowledge of ritual and of all aspects of Buddhism is vast. Furthermore his knowledge is not vague or based on the statements of others; he understands things completely. All his deeds are excellent and

64. A dharani is a type of mantra. Statues are filled with such mantras, which are first tightly rolled so the statue's interior can be filled as fully as possible.

aimed solely at helping others and serving the
teachings.

> Your understanding of all relative knowledge
> is vast.
> In all your good deeds, such as crafts and sewing,
> You help beings and the teachings.
> You delight in the practice of virtue.

Chapter Eight

The Greatness of His Hidden Practice, Faith, and Devotion

(Right to left) Khenpo Karthar Rinpoche, retreat master Tsewang Dorje, Lama Karma Drodül, and others await the arrival of Traleg Rinpoche, Thrangu Monastery, Kham, East Tibet, 2004.

The Greatness of His Hidden Practice, Faith, and Devotion

As regards practice, Rinpoche awakens early every morning and begins to recite mantras using his mala.[65] Wherever he is seated, his posture is erect and his hands remain in a position like Lord Marpa's.[66] Whenever he attends a communal ceremony, he sits up straight. However because he keeps his practice extremely secret, I, a lowly person, do not dare speculate about it.

I've heard Rinpoche's sister Pema Lhakyi say to him many times, "Rinpoche, why do you sit so straight and still when you aren't working? Why don't you recite texts or mantras? Wouldn't that be a better use of your time?"

One day I said something similar to him. Rinpoche responded by telling me the story of a lama who remained in retreat for his whole life at Thrangu

65. A mala is a Buddhist rosary, used to count prayers and mantras.

66. Lord Marpa, the first Tibetan master in the Kagyu tradition, is often depicted seated with the fingertips of his two hands touching the ground in front of his knees. This hand position is called the "earth-pressing gesture," and is said to be the gesture made by (continued)

66. (continued)
the Buddha in
answer to Mara's
challenge to the
Buddha's awaken-
ing. It therefore
represents the
defeat of maras.

67. The four
behaviors are
walking, standing,
sitting, and lying
down.

68. *Author's note*:
Rinpoche received
the complete
empowerments
and teachings
of the Shangpa
Kagyu, including
the six dharmas
of Niguma, from
Kyapjay Kalu
Rinpoche.

68. *Translator's
note*: The eight
masters men-
tioned here are:
the Sixteenth
Gyalwang
Karmapa, Rigpe
Dorje; the Second
Jamgön Rinpoche
of Palpung, Palden
Khyentse Özer;
the Eleventh Tai
Situ Rinpoche,
Pema Wangchok
Gyalpo; Khenpo
Lodrö Rapsal of

Monastery. While telling me the story, Rinpoche quoted the lifelong retreatant as saying, "No matter which of the four behaviors I'm engaged in, I have never strayed from the clear light."[67]

When Rinpoche repeated this to me, I felt absolutely awestruck and thought, "My supreme, kind guru, who has studied under many holy beings, has become just like them! My perception of him has been obscured by thinking of him as an ordinary, familiar person!"

Rinpoche has never identified his root guru by name, but we can infer from many events in his life that Gyalwang Karmapa Rigpe Dorje and Palden Khyentse Özer were his principal teachers. Rinpoche also received the teachings of Tai Situ Pema Wangchok Gyalpo, Shechen Khenpo Lodrö Rapsal, Dilgo Khyentse Rinpoche, Traleg Kyabgön Shedrup Chökyi Nyima, Shechen Kongtrul Rinpoche, Kyapjay Kalu Rinpoche, and other beings on the levels, like the contents of one vase being poured into another.[68] Having received these instructions, Rinpoche, unlike me, has not allowed his being to remain ordinary. He has really achieved the same state of mind as that of his holy masters.

This holy being is a hidden yogin of the true meaning. Even if I declared this with my head held high in a gathering of hundreds or thousands of people, I wouldn't feel a sesame seed's worth of embarrassment, and I say this not because he is my uncle, but in order to express my devotion.

Wherever Rinpoche is staying, he works constantly. He rolls dharanis, fills statues with them, sews the brocade frames for paintings, and makes and affixes drumheads for drums and damarus. He loves to work with his hands.

He treats every disciple he meets with courtesy and affection, touching heads in greeting and so forth. He continually extols the single path trod by all victors and their children: the practice of bodhichitta and mahamudra.

Rinpoche has tremendous devotion for the peerless protectors of beings known throughout the three levels of existence as the Dakpo Kagyu, including Tilopa, Naropa, and all the masters of this lineage. In particular, the Buddha predicted and praised the peerless Gampopa, the source of the ocean of Kagyu siddhas, in many sutras and tantras. In the *Samadhirajasutra*, which teaches mahamudra, it is recounted that Gampopa in a previous life promised the Buddha to spread the mahamudra teachings throughout Tibet, the land of snow-covered mountains. Rinpoche's devotion for Gampopa is so great that tears come to his eyes whenever he hears his name. While teaching *Gampopa's Assembly Dharma*,

68. (continued)

Shechen Monastery; Dilgo Khyentse Rinpoche, one of the principal incarnations of Jamyang Khyentse Wangpo; the previous Traleg Kyabgön Rinpoche, Shedrup Chökyi Nyima; the Second Jamgön Rinpoche of Shechen, Pema Trimay; and Kyapjay Kalu Rinpoche, the activity emanation of Jamgön Kongtrul the Great. The Shangpa Kagyu is the lineage of Khyungpo the Yogin, a Tibetan contempo rary of Marpa, Milarepa, and Gampopa. The six dharmas of Niguma are the Shangpa Kagyu practices that correspond to the Dakpo Kagyu's six dharmas of Naropa. According to Kyapjay Kalu Rinpoche, Niguma was Naropa's sister.

Rinpoche cried like a child amidst large numbers of people. In February of 2005, Rinpoche taught the *Gurusadhana of Gampopa* at Karme Ling, our three-year retreat.[69] He started weeping from devotion three times during his teaching, causing all the retreatants to feel intense devotion and think, "This holy being is an emanation of Gampopa." I know this because we discussed it among ourselves afterwards.

In a newsletter from one of our dharma centers in Michigan, the Sixteenth Gyalwang Karmapa is quoted as saying, "Khenpo Karthar is learned in the practice of the three vehicles. He has all the attributes of a bodhisattva, including great love for everyone."

Once, when Khenpo Rinpoche became ill, one of his disciples asked Tai Situ Rinpoche to compose a prayer for Khenpo Rinpoche's longevity. Situ Rinpoche did so and said, "Don't worry! He has the ability to remain alive for a long time."

Recently when Khenpo Rinpoche entered his eightieth year, Bardor Tulku Rinpoche, who has for almost thirty years worked together with him in enacting the Sixteenth Gyalwang Karmapa's activity, wrote the following, affixed his seal to it, and presented it to Khenpo Rinpoche:

> In auspicious celebration of your eightieth year, I pray from the bottom of my heart that you continue to remain alive for a hundred kalpas for the benefit of beings and the teachings, and that your activity flourish like a river in summer.

69. A sadhana is a liturgical practice used while meditating on a deity. A gurusadhana is a sadhana in which the deity is a guru.

Offered by one called Bardor Tulku on the tenth day of the first month in the Water Sheep Year.

Khenpo Rinpoche, this peerless illuminator of the teachings of the lineage of accomplishment, applying the wondrous practice of luminous mahamudra, continues to open the lotuses of fortunate disciples' minds with the sunlight of his wisdom, leading them to the island of liberation. For thirty years he has, with the utmost kindness, borne the heavy burden of the teachings here as commanded by the Gyalwang Karmapa. For his whole life he has worked for the benefit of beings and the teachings. I cast flowers of joyous praise at him from the depths of my heart.

Whenever he speaks about either the Sixteenth or Seventeenth Gyalwang Karmapa, Khenpo Rinpoche joins his palms in prayer and weeps with devotion. The Seventeenth Gyalwang Karmapa once sent Khenpo Rinpoche a letter, carried by Tendzin Chönyi. This letter was very kind, and included the following:

I pray for your good health, and I join you in dedicating to perfect awakening the virtue of your ceaseless service to the teachings.

Along with the letter, the Gyalwang Karmapa sent Rinpoche a painting and some samaya substances. When Rinpoche received these, he wept visibly, which I saw myself.

On another occasion the Seventeenth Karmapa sent Rinpoche a large photograph of himself. The

70. *Kunga Loter*
means "treasure
of the intellect,
joyous to all."

Karmapa had written on the photo the words "Kunga
Loter" in large letters.[70] There must have been a spe-
cific reason for this, but how could an ordinary person
like me even guess at it?

> Your mind has been mixed with the blessings and
>   quintessential instructions
> Of the victorious father and sons, true buddhas.
> Although there is no difference between
>   meditation and postmeditation for you,
> You are always diligent in gathering great
>   masses of merit.

Chapter Nine
The Greatness of His Wisdom Arisen from Meditation

White Tara torma and shrine, Rinpoche's White Tara retreat,
Karme Ling Retreat Center, 2008.

The Greatness of His Wisdom Arisen from Meditation

Once while traveling to Taiwan with his interpreter Chökyong Palden Radha, Rinpoche sat in meditation for thirteen hours on the airplane. Everyone who saw him was amazed, but because Rinpoche is modest, he claimed that he had been sleeping the whole time.

While Rinpoche was visiting Kaoshung in Taiwan, a woman named Lin Wu Jin Lun, a tailor, offered him a set of robes. Rinpoche then went on to Taipei. While he was there, the tailor suffered a stroke and was hospitalized. Rinpoche was asked to pray for her. The tailor's daughter, who was attending her mother at her bedside, saw our kind guru actually come to the hospital in Kaoshung, be brought to her mother's bedside, and place his hand on her head. He remained there like that for a long time, and then left. The tailor quickly recovered. Delighted, she conveyed her

gratitude to Rinpoche via his interpreter, Chökyong
Palden. Chökyong told her that at the time Rinpoche
had been seen in the hospital in Kaoshung, Rinpoche
was in Taipei, although he had appeared to be meditating. This caused her to feel even more faith and
respect.

Once while Rinpoche was staying at the dharma
center called Kagyu Rangjung Kunkyab in Taiwan, a
young woman who had become possessed by spirits
was brought before him. She started to yell and thrash
about. Rinpoche placed the reliquary he wears
around his neck on top of her head and gave her his
blessing. The young woman soon calmed down, and
repeatedly said, "Thank you!" After awhile she
looked about her in astonishment and asked, "What
am I doing here?" The spirit disturbing her mind had
been pacified. She presented fine offerings in gratitude, and left.

Later our kind guru said, "It was the spirit that
said, 'Thank you' at first. It has left and will harm her
no more. This is through the Gyalwang Karmapa's
compassion!"

One of Rinpoche's disciples is a carpenter named
Clay. While he was building the Ani House at Karme
Ling he worked extremely hard.[71] Our kind guru was
very pleased with him. On a particularly hot day,
when Clay was exhausted by both the hard work and
the terrible heat, he thought about how nice it
would be to drink a cold beer. Thinking that, Clay

71. The Ani House
is a building used
by women for
individual retreats.

walked to the Lama House and sprawled on his bed in exhaustion.[72] He heard someone knocking on his door. When he opened the door, our kind guru walked in and handed him a full bottle of beer. Clay was doubly delighted: by the faith born from thinking, "My guru knows what I'm thinking," and by the beer. Ha, ha!

In 2001 a disciple of Rinpoche's named Michael was diagnosed with untreatable cancer. Just before Michael passed away, Rinpoche went to see him in his hospital room. Michael was breathing with the help of a machine. Soon after arriving, Rinpoche asked everyone else to leave the room, and remained there alone with Michael. Michael removed the breathing apparatus and said that he saw a bright white light. He also told Rinpoche, "I have nothing to worry about; I am ready." He then joined his palms in prayer, his face took on a look of amazement, and he said, "Lord Buddha!" and died. This was definitely due to our kind guru's blessing. Although Michael was a disciple, he had no particular attainment through practice. Nevertheless he had unchanging faith in his gurus and had served our monastery well. Our kind guru says that Michael identified the white and red stages of dissolution.[73]

Long after the passing of the Sixteenth Gyalwang Karmapa, Jamgön Rinpoche visited the United States. One day Jamgön Rinpoche, Khenpo Rinpoche, and others watched a film about the Sixteenth Karmapa's visits to America. The film

72. The Lama House is a building used to host visiting teachers and for individual retreats by men.

73. The white and red stages of dissolution are phases in the dying process. They are often called "white appearance" and "red increase." They are followed by "black attainment" and the "fundamental clear light of death."

included footage of Jamgön Rinpoche. During this, he remarked, "Nothing embarrasses me more than watching myself on film!" He quickly got up from his seat and left the room.

As soon as Jamgön Rinpoche had left the room, our kind guru had the very sad thought, "Jamgön Rinpoche has gone to other realms!" Then he thought, "Jamgön Rinpoche is right here! This inauspicious feeling is unthinkable!" Yet he couldn't shake that feeling of sadness.

Then, after returning to India, Jamgön Rinpoche passed away. Soon after that, while Khenpo Rinpoche was chanting *Calling to the Gurus from Afar* amidst an assembly, he suddenly joined his palms in prayer and wept. Afterward, when his disciples repeatedly asked him why, he said, "Jamgön Rinpoche was really here!" This story was told to me by an American retreat lama named Tsultrim.

Once one of our kind guru's disciples requested that he pray for her brother, who was gravely ill and had been hospitalized for a long time. That night Rinpoche dreamed that someone threw down a blood-stained trident with an iron handle in front of him. On the next day Rinpoche said to both the Taiwanese nun Ani Lodrö and me, "It seems he will die today." The disciple's brother died that night. The disciple called Rinpoche; he performed the ejection of consciousness.

Once when I was about to emerge from retreat, Rinpoche dreamed that he said "Goodbye" in English to the protector lama of Thrangu Monastery in Nepal. Rinpoche told me at the time, "It seems he may pass away soon." A few months later we heard that he had passed away and remained in meditation.

At the end of Rinpoche's visit to Tibet, he departed from Thrangu Monastery by car in order to return to America. A beautiful, large, brown yak with white blazes on its forehead and shoulders came down from the mountains, lowing loudly, right by where Rinpoche's car was driving along the road. Rinpoche says that he immediately thought, "This is definitely the Upasaka!"

In 2004 Rinpoche visited Tibet again, this time accompanied by me and others. While we were re-turning from a trip to Upasaka Bend at Thrangu, a large butterfly with colorful wings appeared, flying in front of our car.[74] It maintained the same speed as our car for a great distance, as though it were escorting us. Rinpoche said that he was certain that the butter-fly was an emanation of the Upasaka.

74. Upasaka Bend is a bend in the road to Thrangu Monastery as it goes past Upasaka Hill, a hill associated with the Thrangu Upasaka.

There are many similar stories I could tell, but I have not received Rinpoche's permission to write about them.

All of these are merely his observable qualities. His truly special qualities are perceivable only by great beings. It is unnecessary to say that they are beyond the thought of an ordinary person like me whose eyes for the sacred are obscured by mundane familiarity.

In the longevity supplication he composed, Kyapjay Situ Rinpoche praises our guru as "learned and accomplished Karma Tarchin." What need is there to say that this is evident to those with unobscured eyes of wisdom?

> Because your mind is indistinguishable from those
>   of the root and lineage gurus,
> You know all things with perfect wisdom.
> Because you are a hidden yogin,
> The ocean of your very secret qualities transcends
>   our intellects.

Chapter Ten
The Greatness of His Creation of Supports and Gathering of Accumulations

His Holiness the Gyalwang Karmapa, tea reception upon arrival at Karma Triyana Dharmachakra, showing the large statue of Buddha Shakyamuni, 2008.

The Greatness of His Creation of Supports and Gathering of Accumulations

Along with Kyapjay Bardor Tulku Rinpoche and Mr. Tendzin Chönyi; and with the assistance of American disciples, Khenpo Rinpoche created the great shrine room at Karma Triyana Dharmachakra. Its central image is a large statue of Buddha Shakyamuni, finely cast of copper and gilded. When it was being filled, Jamgön Rinpoche was present. Khenpo Rinpoche says that Jamgön Rinpoche was extremely pleased by the excellence of the supports, dharanis, and other materials placed within the great statue.[75]

To the right of the central image is a statue of the Sixteenth Gyalwang Karmapa. The dharanis within this statue's head were placed there by Tai Situ Rinpoche. To that statue's right are images of Vajrasattva and Manjushri.

75. Supports are representations of the body, speech, or mind of an awakened being. Supports of body are usually photographs, paintings, or statues. Supports of speech are dharma books and recordings. Supports of mind are stupas and scepters (such as vajras, bells, etc.). These are called "supports" because they support or contain the presence of an awakened person or deity.

76. The Kangyur
and Tengyur
are the Tibetan
editions of the
Buddha's teach-
ings and the
great Indian
commentaries
on them.

To the left of the central image is a stupa containing relics of the Sixteenth Gyalwang Karmapa. It is
made of silver and gold and finely decorated with jewels. To the stupa's left are images of Guru Rinpoche
and White Tara. Our great shrine room also contains
the Kangyur, the Tengyur, parasols, victory banners,
and paintings of the golden garland of Kagyu gurus.[76]

Our library contains the *Five Treasuries* and other
works brought by the Sixteenth Gyalwang Karmapa
from Delhi, including many shastras composed
by the learned and accomplished masters of India and
Tibet.[77] Also in the library are statues of the sixteen
elders.

Our Tara shrine room contains finely cast images of
the twenty-one Taras, various other fine supports, and
countless paintings.

On the second story of the shrine building, in
front, is the lineage shrine room, part of the Gyalwang
Karmapa's private suite. This shrine contains statues
of the golden garland of Kagyu gurus; and a throne,
table, and cushions finely crafted from the best
materials.

All of the canopies, victory banners, and brocades
for the Gyalwang Karmapa's throne; the meditation
cushions for those attending teachings; the brocade
coverings for the altars and thrones; the fabrics used
in elaborate offering and practice assemblies; the
parasols, pennants, and victory banners throughout

the shrine room; and the brocade frames for two sets of paintings of the golden garland of the Kagyu gurus were sewn by our great guru and Bardor Tulku Rinpoche.

They have also given our monastery finely crafted horns, offering lamps, skull cups, mandala plates, and vases, all made of silver and gold, as well as fine cymbals and all the things a monastery should have. They have overseen the choice and creation of all our images and offering vessels.

Once the shrine building was completed, both Rinpoches began to present empowerments, transmissions, and instructions in it; they continue to do so. They have also invited countless gurus of many traditions who have nourished us with the dharma of ripening and liberation.

Every day at our monastery at five AM the *Profound Essence of Tara* and various longevity supplications are chanted. At five PM offerings and supplications to the protectors are chanted along with dedications and aspiration prayers. At seven PM *Benefiting Beings Throughout Space*, the *Amitabha Sadhana*, the *Seven-Line Supplication* with the VAJRA GURU mantra, and longevity supplications are chanted. These are all recited slowly so that meditation and recitation can be coordinated.

Just before the Tibetan New Year the extensive ceremony of the protectors is performed. Every year a

Constructing the shrine building at Karma Triyana Dharmachakra, ca. 1984.

Yeshe Namdak, Tendzin Chönyi, Lama Ganga, Bardor Tulku Rinpoche, Khenpo Karthar Rinpoche, Lama Ugyen, and Lama Norlha, Karma Triyana Dharmachakra, 1978.

78. A yidam is a meditation deity.

weeklong, elaborate accomplishment and offering assembly of one of our three principal yidams — Vajravarahi, Chakrasamvara, and Jinasagara — is held.[78] We also perform yearly an elaborate accomplishment and offering assembly of Amitabha; an offering ceremony commemorating the passing of the Sixteenth Gyalwang Karmapa, Rangjung Rigpe Dorje; a celebration of the Seventeenth Gyalwang Karmapa's birthday; and other ceremonies.

Briefly put, who could fail to cast flowers of praise at our two great resident lineage holders and Mr. Tendzin Chönyi, all of whom would give up their lives for the teachings and the Gyalwang Karmapa? They have, through harmony and pure samaya, created our monastery.[79]

79. Samaya is a practitioner's commitment to their guru and the practice of vajrayana.

The fog of decadent times fills the sky.
Beings, unprotected, suffer terribly.
The Buddha's teachings are at risk.
Yet many great beings of all schools
Compassionately surmount a thousand hardships
In order to help the meek in foreign lands.

80. The Victors' Activity is the Gyalwang Karmapa, who embodies the activity of all buddhas or victors. The two heroes are Khenpo Karthar Rinpoche and Bardor Tulku Rinpoche.

Although the Victors' Activity passed away,
His activity has flourished because of these
    two heroes.[80]
They will never give up, even if it costs their lives.
Their fame fills our world.
These supplementary stanzas just burst forth.

After the Sixteenth Gyalwang Karmapa's passing, it was as though the sun had set behind the western mountains. However every sunset is eventually followed by the sun rising above the eastern peaks. In order to benefit beings and the teachings, the Gyalwang Karmapa was reborn and eventually enthroned at Tsurphu Monastery. Our kind guru and Lama Norlha attended the enthronement. When they first met the Seventeenth Gyalwang Karmapa at his residence, although he was very young, he immediately exhibited his unfluctuating, unobscured wisdom. Smiling, he said to our guru, "Agama, you made it here!"

"Agama" was the term of endearment by which the Sixteenth Karmapa usually addressed Khenpo Rinpoche, which Rinpoche immediately remembered.

There are clear prophecies of the Seventeenth Karmapa by Padmasambhava — the second Buddha — and the great treasure-revealer Chokgyur Lingpa, as well as others. Especially, with clear foreknowledge of the future, the Sixteenth Karmapa entrusted the precious letter predicting his own rebirth to his great heart-son, Tai Situ Rinpoche. Therefore Khenpo Rinpoche was already irreversibly certain about the Seventeenth Karmapa's identity before he met him. Nevertheless what need is there to say that when he actually saw the Seventeenth Karmapa's face, which liberates upon sight, and heard the Gyalwang Karmapa say things that proved his identity,

81. Reliquaries of
this type are worn
as a pendant,
hanging from a
chain or cord that
is worn around
one's neck.

Rinpoche's faith and devotion increased?

At that first meeting, Rinpoche offered the Gyalwang Karmapa a golden reliquary. The Karmapa circumambulated it three times and then put it on.[81] Then the Karmapa said, "Bald old monk, you're very nice to me!"

The hair-cutting ceremony for the Seventeenth Gyalwang Karmapa was held at the Jokhang in Lhasa. Beforehand Tai Situ Rinpoche told Khenpo Rinpoche, "You must hold the Gyalwang Karmapa's crown," and gave it to him.[82]

82. This was the
"daily crown,"
not the actual
Black Crown.

In 1990 when Jamgön Rinpoche visited the United States, he consecrated the land for our three-year retreat facility and exhibited great joy while doing so. Over several years, Khenpo Rinpoche built the men's retreat, which he named Pawo Ling; the women's retreat, which he named Kandro Ling; the Lama House, a residence for visiting masters such as Kyapjay Thrangu Rinpoche and their attendants; and the Ani House, a retreat facility in which nuns and other women can perform independent retreats of varying length.[83]

83. *Pawo Ling*
means "heroes'
park." *Kandro Ling*
means "dakinis'
park." An *ani* is a
Buddhist nun.

The male and female monastics and laypersons who perform our three-year retreats learn written Tibetan beforehand; all of the liturgies used are in Tibetan. The retreatants gather at Karme Ling about three months before their retreat begins, and are instructed by experienced retreatants in written Tibetan and ceremonial practice. During this period,

Kyapjay Thrangu Rinpoche bestows all of the empowerments for the retreat. Then in accordance with Tibetan custom, the retreat begins on the Holy Day of the Descent from Heaven.[84] During the retreat, the gurus invited to our monastery also visit the retreat and bestow teaching, guidance, and blessings. The instructions, transmissions, and practical training are given by our kind guru. He and Lama Tashi Döndrup from Rumtek Monastery have provided detailed explanations of every liturgy and ritual performed in the retreat; these teachings have been recorded and preserved on DVDs and audio CDs. With Khenpo Rinpoche's permission, these recordings have been of great benefit to other retreats, such as Kyapjay Thrangu Rinpoche's retreat in Nepal, Kyapjay Traleg Rinpoche's retreat in Australia, and Kyapjay Trungpa Rinpoche's retreat at Gampo Abbey, Nova Scotia.

Since founding Karme Ling Retreat Center, because of his responsibilities there and his advanced age, Khenpo Rinpoche has delegated the touring of our affiliate centers to Kyapjay Bardor Tulku Rinpoche.

> Although you've crossed the sea of the two
>   accumulations
> You still amass millions of merits in every way that
>   tames beings,
> Such as ripening disciples through the quick path
> And creating supports for our accumulation and
>   purification.

84. The Holy Day of the Descent from Heaven commemorates the Buddha's return to this world after spending a summer teaching his mother's reincarnation in the god realm called Thirty-Three, named after its thirty-three rulers.

Rinpoche and Lama Norlha with retreatants at the beginning of the fourth three-year retreat at Karme Ling Retreat Center, 2004.

Chapter Eleven
The Greatness of His Widespread Activity of Nurturing Disciples Through Empowerment, Transmission, and Instruction

Khenpo Rinpoche and Bardor Tulku Rinpoche with Karma Triyana Dharmachakra residents, 1978.

The Greatness of His Widespread Activity of Nurturing Disciples Through Empowerment, Transmission, and Instruction

The course of practice and instruction in our three-year retreats begins with the mahamudra preliminaries — the four hundred thousand — and the meditation practices of tranquility and insight. All of this takes five months, and is taught based on Jamgön Lodrö Thaye's commentary, *Torch of Certainty*.

The next three months are devoted to the outer, inner, and secret practice of one of three guruyogas: those of Marpa, Milarepa, or Gampopa. Then ten months are spent on the outer, inner, and secret sadhanas of Vajravarahi, taught using the brief guide by Pawo Tsuklak Gyamtso and the long guide by Pawo Tsuklak Trengwa.

Then the six dharmas of Naropa are practiced, starting with their preliminaries, for seven months.

The commentaries used for these practices include *Essence of Amrita* by Shamar Chökyi Wangchuk and several commentaries by Khenchen Karma Ratna: *An Ornament for the Essence of Amrita, A Commentary on the Four Brahmaviharas, A Short Commentary on the Four-Lined Aspiration, A Commentary on the Six Dharmas Supplication, A Brief Commentary on the Supplication Bliss and Emptiness Inseparable, A Commentary on the Four-Lined Aspiration for the Path of Means,* and *Notes on the Four-Session Guruyoga.* Also studied are Karma Chakme's *Notes on the Four-Session Guruyoga*; Palpung Khyentse's commentary on the physical practices, *An All-Illuminating Mirror*; and Karma Chakme's *Ejection: The Hook of Compassion.*

The outer, inner, and secret sadhanas of Chakrasamvara are practiced for eight months, using two commentaries: *A Feast for Yogins' Minds,* composed by Könchok Tendzin, the abbot of Zuru Monastery in Ga and a direct disciple of Jamgön Lodrö Thaye; and Karma Chakme's *Versified Guide to the Five Deities of Chakrasamvara.*

The outer, inner, and secret sadhanas of Jinasagara are practiced for six months. The commentaries used are Drupwang Karma Chakme's guides to the stages of the practice and his essays on its significance.

Every morning the retreatants assemble to recite liturgies including *Renewal and Purification: A Stairway to Freedom.* Every evening they present offerings and supplications to the protectors and burnt offerings. Every day, in their rooms, they offer water torma, cleansing smoke, and severance.[85] All of this is done just as in retreats in Tibet.

Upon the completion of the three yidam practices — Vajravarahi, Chakrasamvara, and Jinasagara — extremely elaborate offering ceremonies and fire offerings are performed. After leaving retreat the lamas continue to perform the mahamudra preliminaries, the daily practices of the three yidams, and the offerings to the protectors every day. Many of them also continue to perform daily the water torma, burnt offering, smoke offering, severance, and physical practices.

Each retreatant contributes US\$17,000. It may sound like a lot of money, but given how expensive it is to live in America, it barely suffices to pay for the food and practice materials each retreatant will need. Offerings of food made to retreatants by the faithful are accepted so that donors may gather the accumulations, but monetary offerings are not distributed to individual retreatants in order to avoid even a whiff of the misuse of sangha funds. About this, our kind guru said, "I am happy knowing that my retreatants are safe from the careless consumption of sangha funds. If money is offered to all the retreatants in common, you may use it for whatever you need as a group." Monetary offerings to our retreats are saved and used for the grateful offering of supports of body, speech,

85. Severance is the well-known practice that was systematized by the great female master Machik Lapdrön.

and mind to our kind guru, and to buy permanent supports for the retreats. Money offered by the faithful to sponsor lamp offerings for the benefit of the living or dead is used to pay for the lamp oil that fuels these very offering lamps.

Khenpo Rinpoche sews all of the shawls, skirts, vests, slips, meditation belts, and exercise skirts worn by the retreatants. At the end of each retreat he sews and presents to each monk and nun a new monastic shawl, skirt, and brocade vest. He similarly sews and presents to each yogin and yogini a new nonmonastic shawl and skirt.

Since its creation, three retreats have been completed at Karme Ling; the fourth is now in session.[86] More than forty lamas have done the three-year retreat there. They are all benefiting beings in their own ways.

Rinpoche's foremost disciple is Lama Yeshe Losal, the brother of Akong Rinpoche. When Lama Yeshe was young he had no interest in dharma and spent his time in wild behavior. He then met the Sixteenth Gyalwang Karmapa, came to the United States, and became a monk. When the Sixteenth Karmapa came to America for the last time and was in Zion, Illinois, displaying to others the appearance of terminal illness, Lama Yeshe was in retreat. He sent everything he had, including about nine thousand dollars, as an offering to the Karmapa. The Karmapa, pleased, jokingly said, "But he hasn't given me his beautiful new

86. The fourth retreat was in session both when this book was written and when it was translated. The retreat ended in February 2008. The fifth retreat began in October 2008.

bed!" Although the Gyalwang Karmapa had never physically seen it, he saw with his unobscured eyes of wisdom the fine new bed that Lama Yeshe had bought.

Lama Yeshe remained in solitary retreat for four years. His diligence in practice was extreme. For example, he performed one million prostrations. As he did them on an uncushioned prostration board, he developed infected sores on his hands and knees. Our kind guru made him a leather pad, and Lama Yeshe wore right through it, leaving two gaping holes where his knees landed on it. Rinpoche says this is a sign that he truly accomplished the result of prostrations.

While practicing chandali during the winter, Lama Yeshe would wash his body outdoors with snow.[87] He also achieved such qualities as stability in tranquility meditation, and is a master of experience and realization. He now lives at Kagyu Samye Ling in Scotland. His activity is vast.

87. Chandali is one of the six dharmas of Naropa.

Another of Khenpo Rinpoche's disciples is the American Lama Karma Wangmo. She first entered the gate of dharma in the presence of the Sixteenth Gyalwang Karmapa. She then asked our kind guru for instruction on Vajravarahi. He told her, "First practice the preliminaries." She went into retreat for a few months in the woods and quickly completed the preliminaries. She then again asked Rinpoche for instruction on Vajravarahi. He told her, "Do a hundred nyungnays and then come back." She did so,

Ngödrup Tsering Burkhar translating for Rinpoche, Columbus, Ohio, 1989.

Chökyong Radha translating for Rinpoche, Karma Triyana Dharmachakra, 1992.

received instruction, and went into solitary retreat for twelve years, during which she devoted herself to the yidam practice of Vajravarahi. Her diligence was tremendous, and there are many stories of her signs of accomplishment. Nowadays she lives without a fixed location as a yogini beyond action.

Another of Rinpoche's disciples is the American Lama Tsultrim. He has completed three group retreats and is now in his fourth. His main practice is Chakrasamvara. The Taiwanese Ani Lodrö has completed two retreats and is now in her third. The American Lama Tsulden completed two retreats. The American Lama Zöpa is now in his second retreat. The Taiwanese Bhikshuni Karuna Lodrö Drönma completed a group retreat and then performed one hundred and eight nyungnays. She is now our nyungnay lama. I, an inferior person, am now pretending to do my second retreat. The Taiwanese Ani Karma Puntsok completed a group retreat, but didn't leave the retreat. She continued to practice Vajravarahi, Chakrasamvara, and Jinasagara until the next group retreat began, which she entered. She is therefore still in retreat, and her main practice is Jinasagara.

Lama Kathy Wesley, also called Jigmay Chötso; Lama Tsultrim Yeshe; Lama Nancy; Lama Tarchin; Lama Lozang; Lama Yeshe Jungnay; Lama Tendzin; Lama Wufang; Lama Pema; and others who have completed retreats reside in many of our affiliate centers. They bestow the vow of refuge, opening the first door to the path of freedom for many men and women in western lands who would otherwise be desperate in their ignorance of right and wrong. Then these lamas gradually lead them on the perfect path in ways appropriate to their individual faculties, such as by presenting the mahamudra preliminaries. Among these lamas, Lama Jigmay Chötso is the most active in touring our affiliate centers and guiding disciples.

Khenpo Rinpoche's disciples who have not done three-year retreats practice the four hundred thousand mahamudra preliminaries and then the *Karma Pakshi Gurusadhana*. These experienced disciples lead assemblies of newer disciples in the practices of Avalokita, Amitabha, and Guru Rinpoche, and also instruct others in the practices of tranquility and insight. Some of Rinpoche's older disciples have also committed themselves to reciting one hundred million MANIs.

The practitioners residing in the Ani House at Karme Ling are not just in retreat for a month or even a year. They are all committed to many years of retreat practice, and some of them to lifelong retreat. One of them, Lama Colleen, is currently practicing the *Embodiment of the Three Jewels* in the Ani House. The men and women who do solitary retreats in the retreat cabin behind our monastery practice such sadhanas as that of Amitabha year after year. Many of Khenpo Rinpoche's Chinese-speaking disciples recited six million Amitabha mantras in the context of the

Amitabha Sadhana to prepare for instruction in the ejection of consciousness. In May 2004, after instructing many of his Chinese-speaking disciples to accumulate the six million mantras, Rinpoche taught them the ejection of consciousness according to the *Sky Dharma* tradition at Karma Yiwong Samten Ling and had them practice it there for a week.[88] As I witnessed myself, most of the disciples achieved signs of ejection.

Our kind guru goes back and forth between our monastery and our retreat center as his teaching responsibilities require. It would be impossible to list everything he has taught at our monastery, but if I merely list his principal teachings, they have included these:

In the summer of 1981 Rinpoche taught the *Amitabha Sadhana* and the *Uttaratantra* for one month. In 1983 for three months he taught the ground, path, and fruition of the mahayana in great detail. In 1984 for several months he taught about the view, meditation, and conduct; and the *Baishajyagurusadhana*. In 1989 and 1990 he taught the *Profound Inner Meaning*. During those two summers the custom of combining ten days of teaching each summer with the celebration of Rinpoche's birthday began. Also, in the fall of 1989 Rinpoche visited Crestone, Colorado to choose and bless the site of our Tashi Gomang Stupa. In 1996 Khenpo Rinpoche, Bardor Tulku Rinpoche, and Bokar

88. Karma Yiwong Samten Ling is the full name of the Karme Ling Retreat Center. It means "Karmapa's Pleasant Meditation Park."

Rinpoche performed the consecration ceremonies for the completed stupa.

In the summer of 1991 Khenpo Rinpoche taught the *Marpa Gurusadhana* for ten days. Since then, summer after summer for ten days each year, he has taught *Mahamudra: The Ocean of Definitive Meaning*, *Mahamudra: Pointing Out the Dharmakaya*, several commentaries on the *Aspiration of Mahamudra*, and Karma Chakme's *Practical Instructions of Great Compassion*.

The Sixteenth Gyalwang Karmapa once told Kyapjay Dezhung Rinpoche that he should teach Karma Chakme's *Mountain Dharma*.[89] As Dezhung Rinpoche subsequently passed into the dharmadhatu, he was unable to comply. Because the Gyalwang Karmapa also remarked to our kind guru that this book needed to be taught, Khenpo Rinpoche taught it in detail to his American disciples. The edited transcripts of Rinpoche's teachings on the *Mountain Dharma* are being published in book form and will comprise five volumes.

89. Kyapjay Dezhung Rinpoche was a great master and eminent scholar of the Sakya tradition.

Khenpo Rinpoche has also taught Atisha's *Beacon on the Road to Awakening* and other shastras; and has bestowed and continues to bestow countless empowerments, transmissions, and instructions, including the cycle *Knowing One Frees All*. Many of his teachings have been published in both English and Chinese as books. One of these, *Dharma Paths*, has been translated into Chinese, French, Hindi, and

Rinpoche and Bardor Tulku Rinpoche, Family Week,
Karma Triyana Dharmachakra, 2001.

other languages and is famous for its great benefit for disciples.

Through his great turning of the profound and vast dharmachakras Khenpo Rinpoche has inspired countless disciples in America, Taiwan, and elsewhere to receive the vow of refuge and then engage in dharma practices that suit their individual capacities, such as the four hundred thousand preliminaries, the *Karma Pakshi Gurusadhana*, and the Avalokita practice. From the longevity supplication by the Seventeenth Gyalwang Karmapa:

> You light the beacon of dharma in a land where it
> was previously absent.
> You bring happiness to the minds of all kinds of
> beings.

Our kind guru is known to have been naturally compassionate from childhood. He is particularly kind to the ill and the poor. He guides his disciples appropriately and affectionately. Everyone, high and low, treats him with great respect. I, a lowly person, have pretended to attend him for several years. During that entire time I have never seen him display anger. He is always relaxed, and always speaks slowly and appropriately. Everything he says is beneficial to others; he never babbles on meaninglessly the way I do. He clearly recollects stories, legends, and even the play of his childhood. No matter whether he is speaking to a highly placed or lowly person, his words always inspire respect. With a smile, he constantly pronounces benedictions such as, "May you be protected by the three jewels!" and "May you be protected by Arya Tara!" All his disciples call him "loving and compassionate." While serving as his interpreter, I have repeatedly heard it said that the mere sight of his face brings joy.

In my own experience, merely seeing his face calms me down when I, an ordinary being, become agitated. He treats the practitioners in our three-year retreats with immeasurable kindness, and assists them with any problems they have such as sickness. He touches heads with them and strokes them like a loving parent. The retreatants often jokingly refer to him in English as "Father" and treat him with measureless respect. It is certain that the awe in which he is held by all of his disciples and their compliance with his instructions are caused by the power of his love and compassion. From the longevity supplication:

> You are always on the path of nonviolence,
> peace, and happiness.

90. The vinaya is the code of moral discipline for Buddhist monks and nuns.

In these evil times, when degeneracy is so widespread, monks who conform to the vinaya are rare.[90] In particular, there are even more impediments to the vinaya in the West than there are elsewhere. Nevertheless this holy being preserves moral discipline independent of others. He is praised for this by everyone, high and low, as I and others have witnessed. In 1998 Khenpo Rinpoche visited Thrangu Monastery in Nepal and took part in the enthronements of Tulku Lodrö Nyima Rinpoche and Tulku Karma Damchö. Khenpo Rinpoche offered them supports, made donations to all the monks, and sponsored the serving of tea to all.

During that visit, Khenpo Tsultrim Namdak from Rapjor Monastery asked Khenpo Karthar Rinpoche to teach on the dohas of Saraha.[91] He responded to the request by saying, "I know nothing about them." When the request was repeated insistently, he responded, "Keep your moral discipline undamaged even at the risk of your life! There is nothing better than that."[92] Khenpo Tsultrim Namdak was amazed and displayed great respect.

When our guru first revisited Thrangu Monastery in Tibet, he served as the abbot for the rainy season retreat. In doing so he restarted the tradition of rainy season retreats there, and it has continued down to the present. During the retreat he spoke strongly to the assembled monks and nuns of the need to preserve moral discipline. It is said:

A bhikshu with moral discipline is luminous.

Accordingly, although our guru is eighty-three years of age, his complexion is radiant. Both his body and clothing emit the fine fragrance of morality. His face has few wrinkles. What need is there to say that these are indications of his extraordinary discipline?

91. The dohas of Saraha are three songs the great master Saraha sang to a king, his queen, and his subjects respectively. These songs are among the most important Indian sources of mahamudra instruction.

92. *Tsultrim Namdak* means "pure morality."

Thrangu Rinpoche and Traleg Rinpoche (front), Lama Tsewang, Khenpo Karthar Rinpoche, Tulku Damchö, Lama Tashi Döndrup, and Lopsang Dorje (back), during Thrangu Rinpoche's visit to Karma Triyana Dharmachakra, 2005.

Teaching *Karma Chakme's Mountain Dharma*, Karma
Triyana Dharmachakra, 2002.

From the longevity supplication:

Holy being with flawless morality, I pray that you
remain.

As is obvious to everyone, these words of praise, written by the Seventeenth Gyalwang Karmapa, reflect
what the Karmapa has seen with eyes of unobscured
wisdom.

In 2001 our kind guru visited India, accompanied
by Bardor Tulku Rinpoche and his wife Sönam, and
by several disciples. They met with the Seventeenth
Gyalwang Karmapa, Ogyen Trinley Dorje, and offered
him a silver mandala piled high with heaps of
turquoise. They attended the great prayer festival of
the Kagyu Mönlam, which was led by the Gyalwang
Karmapa in the company of many of the great masters
of the lineage of accomplishment. Amid this millionfold auspicious splendor revealing the fundamental
inseparability of master and disciples, Bardor
Rinpoche and our kind guru represented Karma
Triyana Dharmachakra Monastery in offering a mandala and supports of body, speech, and mind to the
Gyalwang Karmapa. They also made offerings to others present there including the peerless Kyapjay
Goshri Gyaltsap Rinpoche, Mingyur Rinpoche, Bokar
Rinpoche, and other tulkus and lamas. They made
offerings to the entire assembly of monastics, sponsored a tea service for them all, and gave both money
and food to all the laypeople present.

Long before that visit to India, Khenpo Rinpoche's knees had deteriorated to a point where they were in no condition for him to be seated cross-legged for long periods of time. Nevertheless he sat cross-legged throughout the entire Mönlam festival, which he later admitted to me required considerable forbearance. When he returned from India, his knees had improved greatly.

None of the monetary or other offerings our guru receives from donors ever go to waste; he ensures that they are all used for the creation of supports or other dharmic purposes. He has always used the donations he receives to sponsor the building of our retreats, the installation of images, and such things; he continues to do so. He has also assisted Rumtek Monastery, Kyapjay Thrangu Rinpoche's monasteries, and other Kagyu monasteries by sponsoring their facilities and images.

Through the current of empowerment,
    transmission, and instruction,
You ripen and free beings, placing each
    appropriately on the three yanas' path.
Your activity is tremendously vast, including
    direct and indirect disciples.
You free your mothers born in foreign lands
    from the ocean of becoming.[93]

93. This line refers to the Buddhist belief that all beings have been one's mother.

His Holiness the Sixteenth Gyalwang Karmapa, Black Crown
Ceremony, Rumtek, Sikkim, ca. 1977.

Chapter Twelve

The Greatness of His Fulfillment of His Guru's Commands

The Eighth Traleg Kyabgön Rinpoche, 1901-1953.

The Greatness of His Fulfillment of His Guru's Commands

On June 5th and 6th, 2004, our guru bestowed instructions on the bardo and a longevity empowerment in one of our nearby affiliate centers. At the conclusion of his teachings and empowerment, he was asked what disciples could do to preserve the longevity of their guru. His principal advice was that the longevity of gurus depends mainly upon the purity of samaya disciples maintain toward one another and their fulfillment of their guru's commands. After saying that, Rinpoche told the following story:

"While the Sixteenth Gyalwang Karmapa was visiting the United States, he said to me, 'In order to support the dharma practice of disciples, build a monastery of whatever size you can. As there is as yet no place to put the many texts I have given to the future monastery, and as you are presently storing them in the garage, the monastery you build must have a library. Teach and transmit the writings of the previous Kagyus to disciples in our centers. Have disciples who have completed the four hundred thousand preliminaries practice the *Karma Pakshi Gurusadhana*; it is a very important practice because it is a means of accomplishing the gurus, yidams, and dharmapalas indivisibly.'

"Then the Gyalwang Karmapa said to me, as though he were joking, 'You need to put extremely diligent disciples into three-year retreat, so it would be good if you could also build a retreat for the six dharmas of Naropa!'

"I worried that I lacked the ability to do this. Later we acquired a large piece of land in New Mexico. I planned to build our retreat there. I asked Lama Ganga, 'If I undertake the responsibility to build a retreat, would you be willing to be the resident retreat master?'

"He seemed very pleased, and answered, 'That would be fine.'

"As it turned out, however, the land in New Mexico was unsuitable and Lama Ganga soon passed away; there was nothing to be done. Nevertheless through the Gyalwang Karmapa's compassion, we were eventually able to build our retreat at Karme Ling and many retreat lamas have been trained there. Although my disciples are not very learned in scripture and reasoning, they all practice dharma and behave with modesty. In particular, as the Gyalwang Karmapa commanded, we are all practicing dharma purely without polluting it with even a hair-tip's worth of politics. I have fulfilled the commands given personally to me by the Gyalwang Karmapa."

From the longevity supplication:

> With unfabricated faith you obey your guru's
> commands.
> You are constantly and devotedly diligent in
> teaching and accomplishment.

The meaning of those words can be easily ascertained from the various sections of this biography. In his longevity supplication for our guru, Kyapjay Thrangu Rinpoche wrote:

> Through the blessings of all victors' compassion
> And the power of our purely good intentions
> May this completer of the activity
> Of the glorious Gyalwang Karmapa live long.[94]

This prayer has proven meaningful.

> You devotedly raised the victory banner of the
> commands
> Of the Gyalwang Karmapa, the Lord of Snow
> Mountains.
> You courageously spread the teachings of
> accomplishment to the ten directions.

94. The word *completer* is a translation of the Tibetan word *tarchin*, which can mean both "perfected" and "one who perfects." It is part of Khenpo Karthar Rinpoche's name; "Karthar" is an abbreviation of "Karma Tarchin."

Your obedience to the victors' commands is
honored by devas and humans.

In 2002 Tsewang Lhamo, a professor from the
Minorities' University in Beijing who wrote a treatise
on Tibetan language and culture called *A New
Magnifying Glass on Culture*, visited the United
States. She had previously met our kind guru once in
India, on which occasion she had said to him, "I have
heard a great deal about you; I feel fortunate to final-
ly meet you!" When she visited America, Tsewang
Lhamo served as Rinpoche's interpreter on several
occasions. When she was about to leave the United
States, she said to him, "I may never see you again!"
Sobbing, she clasped his feet.

Rinpoche consoled her, saying, "We will meet
again." When he went to Tibet in 2004, Rinpoche visited Beijing. While there he met with her twice, and
she offered him a silver cup and other things.

In 2003, in response to the request of Lama Nyima,
Rinpoche encouraged donors and disciples to con-
tribute to the restoration of Marpa's residence at
Drowolung in Lhodrak. In that way Rinpoche assisted
in the restoration of the buildings and their contents.
Kyapjay Bardor Tulku Rinpoche and our kind guru
have over the years provided great assistance to
Rumtek Monastery, financial and otherwise, and continue to do so.

In August of 2004 our kind guru went to Tibet
with about thirty disciples to attend the opening

ceremonies for the new temple at Thrangu Monastery. On the way he made offerings to Kumbum Monastery and performed a Vajravarahi ganachakra at Blue Lake, a place associated with the accomplishment of Vajravarahi.[95]

When Rinpoche arrived at Thrangu he was welcomed by an elaborate procession. During the opening ceremonies he contributed greatly to the temple's supports and sponsored offerings to all present. He stayed there for seven days, during which time he fulfilled the hopes of all the devoted monastics and laypeople who came to see him, encouraging their dharma practice and giving them blessed supports. He had brought with him two hundred small silver reliquaries, each containing one of the Gyalwang Karmapa's black pills as well as one of the pills prepared from the previous Karmapa's blood. Rinpoche gave these reliquaries to those who came to see him. Rinpoche instructed each person who received one of the reliquaries that they should recite one hundred million MANIs and recollect death and impermanence.

Rinpoche was invited by the khenpos and retreat masters to teach in Thrangu Monastery's six dharmas of Naropa retreat and in its college. He lectured extensively on the four dharmas of Gampopa.[96] All the lamas and monks of Thrangu Monastery together offered Rinpoche supports of body, speech, and mind.

The following is a summary of Rinpoche's address to the assembled monastery:

95. A ganachakra is a type of tantric offering ceremony.

96. The four dharmas of Gampopa are Lord Gampopa's famous summary of the spiritual path of Buddhism: one's mind going to the dharma, dharma becoming a path, the path dispelling delusion, and delusion arising as wisdom.

With Jamgön Rinpoche at Rinpoche's birthday celebration, Karma Triyana
Dharmachakra, ca. 1986-87.

Consecration ceremony, Karma Thegsum Tashi Gomang Stupa, Crestone, Colorado, 1996.

Since I first became a monk of Thrangu Tashi Chöling Monastery I have never quarreled with any of its monks, younger or older. I have maintained the pure discipline of harmony with all. Through the good fortune of my making a slight connection with study and practice at Thrangu Monastery and through the compassion of the Gyalwang Karmapa I moved to the United States of America, a country with a language, customs, and culture radically different from our own. Nevertheless through the blessing of the study and practice of holy dharma, I have been able to establish about six thousand American disciples in dharma. I therefore ask all of you who have access to the favorable conditions of this monastery's college and retreat to not waste your present freedom and resources. I ask you to study, reflect, meditate, and practice.

Rinpoche then visited the sacred image of Vairochana and recited the renewal and purification ceremony called *Stairway to Freedom* with his foreign retreat lamas. He then blessed about one hundred nuns who were there on pilgrimage. Then Khenpo Rinpoche, Lodrö Nyima Rinpoche, and the disciples went to Mount Wu Tai Shan, where they visited all the sacred sites there and presented elaborate offerings.[97] Rinpoche taught an assembly there of about eight hundred Chinese nuns, with Ani Lodrö translating.

In February of 2005 Khenpo Rinpoche prepared for the Tibetan New Year as in years past, making tor-

97. Mount Wu Tai Shan is a five-peaked mountain in China that is said to be the dwelling place of the bodhisattva Manjushri in this world.

mas, setting out offerings, creating the ceremonial flour and butter, and engaging in all the preparations required by Tibetan tradition. He performed the year's end protector ceremonies with other lamas and monks and then enjoyed the New Year festivities. In March he returned to our retreat at Karme Ling and taught us the *Gurusadhana of Gampopa*. During this time he continued to prepare samaya substances and especially many pills made from the Gyalwang Karmapa's blood. He also sewed new covers for the many volumes of the *Treasury of Precious Revelations*.[98]

At the beginning of April he returned to Karma Triyana Dharmachakra Monastery and resumed his ongoing teaching programs. He completed his explanation of Jonang Taranatha's commentary on the *Aspiration to Excellent Conduct* and began to teach the *Aspiration of Maitreya*. Around the middle of that month he returned to Karme Ling and resumed the rolling of dharanis and his sewing, both of which he did in the basement of the Lama House. At the end of the month he spent two days teaching a few lamas who had finished the three-year retreat how to perform the Amitabha funeral ceremony.

At the beginning of May the interpreter Chungda stayed at the Lama House for several days in order to ask Rinpoche questions about his teachings on *Gampopa's Assembly Dharma*, which Chungda was translating into Chinese. At the same time Rinpoche's

98. This is the largest of the *Five Treasuries* of Jamgön Kongtrul the Great.

disciple Bhikshuni Karuna Lodrö Drönma completed one hundred and eight nyungnays. An audiotape of Rinpoche's brother Lama Sönam arrived from Nepal. In it, Lama Sönam said that he had recited more than one hundred million MANIs but intended to remain in retreat, and that he had sponsored the carving of images of the Buddha to decorate the columns at the temple on the site where the Buddha in a past life fed his body to a starving tigress.

Rinpoche was delighted by his brother's news and recorded a lengthy response in which he said, "Your recitation of MANIs and your lifelong retreat are the best way to benefit beings and repay the kindness of our parents and our deceased brothers. As commanded by the Gyalwang Karmapa, I live here. I only pretend to practice while I consume the food of the sangha. Nevertheless I regard all money I receive as the property of the three jewels and always spend it on the creation of supports. I never keep it myself, so my mind is at ease."

Rinpoche then returned to Karma Triyana Dharmachakra, where he continued to teach the *Aspiration of Maitreya* and also bestowed a Tara empowerment on more than a hundred people. He then visited the Gyalwang Karmapa's New Jersey center with Bardor Rinpoche and consecrated a new Medicine Buddha shrine there. This was attended by about two hundred and fifty people. Khenpo Rinpoche then visited Chuang Yen Monastery, a large

Chinese Buddhist temple complex, where for two days he taught *Mahamudra: The All-Sufficient Virtue* by Kyapjay Kalu Rinpoche and also bestowed the upasaka vows.

Khenpo Rinpoche returned then to Karme Ling, where he taught Karma Chakme's *Mountain Dharma* for one week to Chinese-speaking disciples with the help of the Taiwanese interpreter Sönam Lhundrup. Then Rinpoche gave his Taiwanese disciple Judy Chen, who had completed the third three-year retreat held at Karme Ling, further individual instruction on the preliminaries to the six dharmas of Naropa. This was also translated by Sönam Lhundrup.

At the beginning of June, Khenpo Rinpoche visited Kyapjay Thrangu Rinpoche's retreat center in Colorado, where he bestowed the ripening empowerments of the Medicine Buddha and White Tara and the liberating instructions from Tsele Natsok Rangdröl's *Stainless Beacon: An Explanation of Mahamudra.* Then Kyapjay Mingyur Rinpoche visited Karme Ling and bestowed the transmission and guidance of *Mahamudra: Pointing Out the Dharmakaya* for three days.

At the end of June and until the Fourth of July, Khenpo Rinpoche taught Karma Chakme's *Practical Instructions* for ten days at KTD.[99] During this time more than a hundred disciples gathered to celebrate Rinpoche's birthday. Immediately after, Rinpoche led an assembly of about fifteen retreat lamas in a

99. KTD is an acronym for Karma Triyana Dharmachakra.

Stupas offered by Rinpoche's students for Rinpoche's long life, Thrangu Monastery, Kham, East Tibet, 2004.

Rinpoche at Thrangu Monastery with Lama Karma Drodül and the women's retreat master, Kham, East Tibet, 2004.

100. Garchen Rinpoche is one of the greatest living masters of the Drikung Kagyu, one of the twelve branches of the Dakpo Kagyu.

101. The four noble truths were the subject of the Buddha's first sermon. They are the truth of suffering, the truth of the cause of suffering, the truth of the cessation of suffering, and the truth of the path to that cessation.

102. Karma Thegsum Chöling, "Karmapa's Dharma Park of the Three Vehicles," is the name given to the centers affiliated with Karma Triyana Dharmachakra Monastery. There are currently twenty-seven of these centers, and they are situated throughout the United States. In addition to these, there are two other affiliates: Karme Ling Retreat Center in Delhi,

weeklong Chakrasamvara accomplishment and offering ceremony at the monastery. Very pleased with how well it went, Rinpoche returned to Karme Ling. Garchen Rinpoche, invited to our retreat center, spent a day at the Lama House and blessed the men's and women's retreats.[100]

At the same time Khenpo Rinpoche received a taped message from his sister Pema Lhakyi telling him that she had completed two hundred million MANIs, which delighted him. He continued his usual constant work at the retreat making reeds for the gyalings, the horns used in ceremonies.

On the eighth of August, Khenpo Ugyen Tendzin from Rumtek Monastery gave his first teaching at KTD, an explanation of the four noble truths.[101] Khenpo Karthar Rinpoche attended this, offered Khenpo Ugyen a mandala, and opened the door of auspiciousness. Then our guru continued his previous series of teachings at KTD by beginning to explain the aspiration from the *Bodhicharyavatara*. As KTD had by then received permission from the Town of Woodstock to build its new residential and guest quarters, Bardor Tulku Rinpoche, Khenpo Tsultrim Gyamtso Rinpoche, Khenpo Karthar Rinpoche, and Khenpo Ugyen blessed the construction site.

At the beginning of September Kyapjay Traleg Rinpoche visited the New York City Karma Thegsum Chöling and taught the four dharmas of Gampopa.[102]

He then visited Karma Triyana Dharmachakra.

After teaching there, he went on to Karme Ling, where he stayed for two days. He visited both the men's and women's retreats and spoke to the retreatants about bodhichitta. By the time of Traleg Rinpoche's visit, as commanded by our kind guru I had input into my computer the existing biography of Nyima Tashi, the First Traleg Rinpoche, as well as brief biographies of his subsequent incarnations dictated to me by Khenpo Rinpoche. I showed what I had done to both Khenpo Rinpoche, who wept with joy, and Traleg Rinpoche, who was also pleased.[103]

Khenpo Rinpoche then returned to KTD, where he continued to teach the aspiration from the *Bodhicharyavatara*. He then visited a dharma center for Chinese speakers in New York City, where he bestowed the empowerment of Akshobhya. He then returned to Karme Ling, where we were about to begin the inner sadhana of Vajravarahi. In previous retreats everyone had used crossed dharma-sources made from wood.[104] Khenpo Rinpoche made beautiful ones for us out of copper. He also began cutting wood in preparation for the concluding fire offering. On the day we began the inner sadhana he visited both retreats and performed the necessary blessings, including the generation and merging of the mandalas.

At the beginning of October Rinpoche went to KTD and filled Mr. Trinley Chöjor's new statues with dharanis. He then visited the Hartford, Connecticut Karma Thegsum Chöling, where he taught *Gampopa's*

102. (continued) New York; and the Karma Thegsum Tashi Gomang Stupa in Crestone, Colorado.

103. This biography has been translated and published by KTD Publications as *Nyima Tashi*.

104. A dharma-source can be either a triangle or a tetrahedron. In either case it represents the dharmadhatu and the three gates of liberation: emptiness, absence of characteristics, and absence of desire. When crossed or doubled, the dharma-source also represents the transcendence of samsara through wisdom and of nirvana through compassion. Crossed dharma-sources are used in the rituals performed at Karme Ling Retreat Center.

Assembly Dharma. Rinpoche returned to KTD, where he taught the *Sukhavati Aspiration* by the Fifth Gyalwang Karmapa and bestowed the empowerment of White Tara.

On November 21st, Kyapjay Bardor Tulku Rinpoche emerged from a monthlong personal Yamantaka retreat and bestowed the empowerment of that deity at Kunzang Palchen Ling. Khenpo Rinpoche attended the day's events and received the empowerment.

At the beginning of December Khenpo Rinpoche went to KTD and continued to teach the *Sukhavati Aspiration.* He then returned to Karme Ling and told us joyfully, "I have just heard from Druppön Rinpoche that the US$200,000 dollars Bardor Rinpoche and I offered for the construction of a new retreat at Rumtek Monastery were saved for that purpose, and that the construction of the retreat will be soon completed."[105]

105. Druppön Rinpoche is the general secretary of the Seventeenth Gyalwang Karmapa.

Soon after that a disciple of Rinpoche's named Cal, an older man who had been ill for some time, passed away. Just before Cal's death Rinpoche told me, "Last night I dreamed of an old dog that was tethered by a leash. I felt sorry for it and thought to myself, 'I must buy this dog.' The dog's owner was a monk; I asked him the dog's price. He told me the dog cost US$480,000. While I was thinking 'That's cheap!' the dog ran off, leaving only the leash in my hand. I awoke from the dream feeling sad. I think this means Cal is going to die."

Observing that in America the ashes of those who are cremated are often cast into bodies of water, Rinpoche has built a columbarium at Karme Ling for the use of his disciples and others who have expressed interest. The value of the columbarium lies in Rinpoche's dedication to the benefit of all interred there. Both the retreats at Karme Ling perform daily singed offerings and prayers for the deceased; all the tulkus and lamas invited to Karme Ling perform prayers for those whose remains have been placed there; and offering lamps are burnt daily for their benefit. The columbarium contains about three hundred niches for the placement of ashes. Its construction was directed by Lama Karma Lodrö, the manager of Karme Ling. The columbarium's main images include statues of the buddhas of the five families and the eight great bodhisattvas. These were ordered from Nepal by our kind guru, who also went to great trouble in order to fill them with the appropriate dharanis.

In these ways our kind, holy guru continues at the age of eighty-three to uphold the great burden of the buddhadharma and especially the Kagyu teachings.[106] In spite of his age, the marks and signs of his body remain resplendent and his lotus feet are firmly planted on the golden throne of his activity.

To supplement this account, I will briefly explain

106. Rinpoche was eighty-three when this book was translated in 2007.

107. Mahavajra-
dhara means
"great
Vajradhara."

the benefits of recollecting the wondrous qualities of the supreme, glorious guru Mahavajradhara's three secrets and all his kindness; praying to him with fierce devotion; presenting offerings to him; and praising him.[107]

107. Mahavajra-
dhara means
"great
Vajradhara."

The guru is the source of all happiness and goodness, the root of all paths, the increaser of all virtue, the great physician who heals all sickness from the three poisons, and the holy guide who brings us

108. The three
poisons are
desire, hatred,
and delusion.

across the ocean of existence.[108] He is like the sun in that he destroys the darkness of ignorance. He is learned, noble, and benevolent. Through hearing, thinking, and meditating; teaching, debate, and composition; and explanation, accomplishment, and work, he upholds, guards, and spreads the teachings. His activity is as vast as space. Based on the precious, pure morality that pleases the noble ones, he is filled with love, compassion, and precious bodhichitta. He is able to transmit the natural connate vajra

109. Natural con-
nate vajra wisdom
is the wisdom of
awakening.

wisdom to the continuums of disciples.[109] He is the victor Vajradhara appearing as a flesh-and-blood human being.

From the *Sutra of Stainless Space*:

> Ananda, tathagatas do not appear to all beings. Spiritual friends do appear to all beings. They teach dharma and plant the seed of liberation. Therefore regard spiritual friends as greater than tathagatas.

From the *Samvarodayatantra*:

> The guru is the buddha. The guru is the dharma.
> The guru is also the sangha.

As taught countless times in all sutras and tantras, the compassion and kindness of the root guru is far greater than those of all the buddhas and bodhisattvas of the three times. We do not have the good fortune to meet other buddhas or bodhisattvas. We have fallen into the inexhaustible ocean of samsara and experience unceasing suffering. Nevertheless through the compassion of the glorious guru who is a perfect buddha, we have acquired a precious human body with its freedom and resources. We have met with the precious teachings of the victor. We have everything we need to practice dharma. We employ our three gates in virtue. We have faith in the three jewels and believe in karma.

Our guru shows us the two precious bodhichittas. In particular, he directly points out mahamudra. Even if the Buddha appeared to us there would be nothing more than this for him to do. In brief, although our guru is the equal of all buddhas in qualities, his kindness is far greater than that of all buddhas. Our development of any tiny quality and our removal of any tiny fault are due to our guru's kindness.

O, yet I and others like me — disciples whose eyes of faith are obscured — think, "Although my knowledge of holy dharma is due to my guru's kindness, my

wealth, luxuries, and reputation have arisen due to
my own ability." We are proud and vain. Even when
we offer something trivial to our guru, we do so with
the hope of getting something good in return. If our
guru doesn't acknowledge our offering, we frown with
displeasure. Forgetting that we practice dharma for
our own good, we boast of even the slightest austerity.
Especially we foment jealousy and distrust among our
fellow disciples. Our eyes of pure appearance are
obscured. Because we have accompanied our guru for
a long time, our faith and samaya have become adul-
terated. If we give rise to some glimpse of meditation
experience, we forget that even this is due to our
guru's kindness. Thinking that we are realized, we
carry the view in our mouths. We perceive our guru,
who gives us so many profound instructions, as no
more than our peer. These are certain signs that the
devaputramara has entered our hearts.[110] It is unnecessary to say that everything good in the world and
beyond it is due to the kindness of our guru, our spiritual friend. We must also regard physical sickness,
mental suffering, enemies, lawsuits, and everything
undesirable or harmful as our guru's compassionate
encouragement to practice holy dharma.

   Although when we are happy and comfortable we
seem to have faith, as soon as the slightest adversity
arises we fall under its power and are left with an
untrained continuum. This exposes our failure to
both understand the point of dharma and to practice

110. The
devaputramara
is the mara that
is the child of
the gods. In the
most general
terms, a mara
is anything that
impedes the
achievement of
full awakening.

it. Jamgön Kongtrul wrote a great deal about this, such as:

> Externally we look like perfect Buddhists.
> Internally our minds are unmixed with dharma.
> Like poisonous snakes we harbor our kleshas.
> Amidst adversity the faults of Buddhists are
>   displayed.

And:

> We look like Buddhists when our bellies are full
>   and the sun is warm.
> When adversity arises we are just ordinary people.

In brief, although countless buddhas and bodhisattvas have appeared, there remain many wild and decadent beings like me that have not been tamed. Our precious guru shows his face to such beings and cares for us with great affection. He is kinder to us than all buddhas. Without regard for your body or life, engage solely in what pleases him. Avoid doing anything displeasing to him for even an instant. If you come into conflict with him because of previous karma or present circumstances, be certain to confess your fault both directly and indirectly.[111] Resolve that your guru is free of any fault, has every quality, and is the dharmakaya Vajradhara.

We can put up with trying to be pleasing, generous, and obedient to people on whom we must depend in order to achieve minor mundane aims. We will

111. In this case, a direct confession is a confession made to the guru, and an indirect confession is a confession made while praying and meditating by oneself.

Rinpoche with His Holiness the Seventeenth Gyalwang Karmapa, Karma Thegsum Chöling, New Jersey, 2008.

Rinpoche and Tendzinla as His Holiness the Dalai Lama leaves Karma Triyana Dharmachakra, September, 2006.

depend and rely on our guru, however, until awakening. He is our protector, refuge, and support. If you think, think about his deeds. If you speak, speak of his qualities. In meditation, mix your mind and his. In postmeditation, cultivate his pure appearance. Always cultivate devotion and pray. Regard whatever he does as good. Take whatever he says to be true. Know whatever happens to be his blessing and siddhi. Especially it is taught that our tradition, the Dakpo Kagyu, is the lineage of devotion. As for the benefits of devotion to the guru, this is written in the tantras:

112. The completion stage is the second of the two stages of vajrayana practice. The first stage is the generation stage. The main generation stage practices for the Karma Kagyu are the deity practices done in the Karme Ling three-year retreat. The main completion stage practices for the Karma Kagyu are mahamudra and the six dharmas of Naropa, both of which are also practiced in the three-year retreat.

It is better to undistractedly imagine the guru's
   form
Than to meditate on the bodies of a hundred
   thousand deities.
The second does not equal a hundred-thousandth
   of the first.
It is better to diligently pray to the guru three times
Than to recite millions and billions of mantras.
The second does not even approach a
   hundred-thousandth of the first.
It is better for the guru to just appear within your
   mind
Than to meditate on the completion stage for a
   kalpa.[112]
The second does not equal a twenty-thousandth
   of the first.

And:

> It is better to briefly recollect the guru
> Than to meditate on a deity with marks and signs
> For a hundred thousand kalpas.
> The merit of remembering the guru is infinite.

The Fourteenth Gyalwang Karmapa Tekchok Dorje wrote:

> As we Dakpo Kagyupas follow the lineage of devotion mahamudra, whenever we meditate on any of the three roots we meditate that the deity, whatever its appearance, is indistinguishable from our root guru in nature.[113] It is through our relying solely on this instruction — the all-sufficient virtue of devotion — that this land of Tibet has overflowed with siddhas from the time of Lords Marpa, Mila, and Gampopa down to the present.

113. The three roots are the gurus, the root of blessing; the meditation deities, the root of attainment; and the dharma protectors, the root of activity.

Jamgön Lodrö Thaye wrote endlessly about this. For example:

> Devotion is our inheritance from the ocean of Kagyu siddhas. It is the quintessence of the path of secret mantra. It is what all faithful kusalis practice.[114] Especially it is the most precious jewel of Naropa's Kagyu. Recognize devotion to the guru to be your most precious jewel, and instruct others accordingly.

114. A kusali is a yogin or yogini whose lifestyle is of the utmost simplicity.

And:

> Whatever vajrayana practice you do, and especial-
> ly whatever completion stage instructions you prac-
> tice, you must take your guru's blessings as the
> path. Without his blessings entering you, the gen-
> uine path will not arise within you. It is taught that
> if a disciple with samaya has heartfelt devotion for
> a qualified vajra master, that disciple will attain
> both the supreme and common siddhis even if they
> lack any other method. If you lack devotion for
> your guru, even if you complete the mantra recita-
> tions for every yidam of the four tantras you will
> definitely not attain supreme siddhi.[115]

And:

> If genuine devotion arises within you, all correction,
> enhancement, and supreme and common siddhis
> will be achieved without the need to depend on
> anything else. That is why we call this "the pro-
> found path of guruyoga."

And:

> Through devotion, realization will arise of itself.
> Through devotion, awareness will awaken in your
> heart. Through devotion, you will see self-aware-
> ness as the dharmakaya. Through devotion, you
> will see all that appears and exists as the guru.
> Through devotion, deluded projection will stop
> suddenly. Through devotion, wind and mind will

115. The four
tantras are four
levels or types of
vajrayana practice.
They are action
tantra, perform-
ance tantra, yoga
tantra, and highest
yoga tantra. The
practices done in
the Karme Ling
three-year retreat
are derived from
highest yoga
tantra.

enter the avadhuti. Through devotion, appearances and mind will mix into one taste. Through devotion, wrongdoing and downfalls will be naturally purified. Through devotion, you will recognize appearances and sounds as deities and mantra. Through devotion, all nondharmic thoughts will be pacified. Through devotion, you will be liberated from all obstructors and errors. Through devotion, you will easily and quickly traverse the paths and stages. Through devotion, through knowing one thing, all things will be liberated for you.

For devotion to be authentic, four things are needed. You must never examine the guru's faults. You must know that whatever he does is good. You must resolve upon the cessation of hope and fear. You must think of the guru as a parent.

If you see the guru as a buddha, you will receive a buddha's blessing. If you see him as a bodhisattva, you will receive a bodhisattva's blessing. If you see him as a siddha, you will receive a siddha's blessing. If you see him as an ordinary spiritual friend, you will receive the blessing of an ordinary spiritual friend. If you have no devotion, you will receive no blessing. Therefore all blessing and siddhi depend upon the presence or absence of devotion for your guru. Devotion comes from a correct understanding of your guru's deeds and the recollection of his kindness. The interdependence of these can be ascertained from the words of the victor Vajradhara.

The author and Rinpoche at Moon Sun Hill, Kham, East Tibet, 2004.
In the time of King Trisong Deutsen this was the border between Tibet and China.
The Chinese princess, Wencheng, was traveling to Tibet to become the bride of the
king. She was extremely upset until she arrived at this border. Upon receiving a
gau, her sadness disappeared and she was confident that she would be happy as
King Trisong Deutsen's queen.

A hut near the Vairochana retreat house, Thrangu Monastery, Kham, East Tibet, 2004.

From the tantras:

> The vajra master is omniscient.
> He is the wish-fulfilling jewel of omniscient
>   wisdom.
> The guru's long and short biographies
> Are the basis of strong devotion.
> They are like wish-fulfilling jewels.
> There is no doubt that those who repeatedly
>   and diligently
> Study them will achieve siddhi.

The benefits of praying to your guru with genuine devotion are immeasurable. Lord Götsangpa said:[116]

> They are infinite.
> If summarized, they are the following:
> A benefit of prayer is
> Mixing your mind with your guru's.
> A benefit of prayer is
> The arising of uncommon realization.
> A benefit of prayer is
> Unceasing meditation experience.
> A benefit of prayer is
> Being always protected by the three jewels'
>   compassion.
> A benefit of prayer is
> The spontaneous accomplishment of whatever
>   you want or need.
> A benefit of prayer is
> That dakinis and dharmapalas will see you as
>   their child.

116. Götsangpa was a great master of the Drukpa Kagyu, one of the twelve branches of the Dakpo Kagyu.

Geshe Dromtönpa said:

> I have experienced that the blessing of praying to Atisha is greater than the blessing of praying to yidam deities.

It is also taught that the benefits of seeing the form body of your immeasurably kind root guru, Mahavajradhara, even once are infinite. From the *Gandavyuha*:

> Seeing the spiritual friend is the source of all precious qualities. It is the cause of the purification and perfection of all bodhisattva deeds. It purifies all thought. It brings you into the mandala of retention. It generates the light of samadhi. It accomplishes the seeing of buddhas. It sends down a rain of buddhadharmas.

Padampa Sangyay said:

> There is more benefit in seeing the guru's face even once than in seeing the faces of a hundred yidam deities, yet foolish Tibetans fail to understand this.

The benefits of thinking of the guru even once are also infinite. From the *Radiant Wisdom Beacon Tantra*:

> Someone who thinks for an instant of the body of a deity adorned by the marks and signs accumulates more merit than someone who gives generously,

guards morality, cultivates patience, practices diligence, rests in meditation, and generates wisdom
for eighty-four thousand kalpas. Someone who
thinks of their guru for an instant accumulates
more merit than someone who meditates on the
body of a deity adorned by the marks and signs for
eighty-four thousand kalpas. Why? Because they
will attain buddhahood in that very life.

From the *All-Inclusive Wisdom Assembly*:

> The merit of recollecting the guru is infinite,
> Greater than that of meditating
> On a hundred thousand deities
> For a hundred thousand kalpas.

From the *Pungzang Kriyatantra*:

> If when someone dies
> They recollect their guru for a moment,
> This is the best transference of consciousness.
> That person will achieve manifest buddhahood.

As for the benefits of creating images of the glorious
guru and presenting offerings and praise, from the
Tantra of the Array of Ati:

> It is better to paint a single image of the guru
> Than to fill all the world with countless images
> Of innumerable buddhas cast from gold
>   and silver.
> The second does not equal a hundredth,

A thousandth, a ten-thousandth,
Or a hundred-thousandth of the first.
There is more merit in presenting
Offerings and praise to an image of the guru
Than in presenting offerings and praise
To Vajradhara for a hundred kalpas.
The second does not equal one thirty-fifth
Of one hundred-thousandth of the first.

Also, as for the benefits of posthumous offerings to the glorious and peerlessly kind guru, from the *Tantra of the Recognition of the Guru's Qualities*:

If you present offerings with yearning upon your
    guru's passing
Your virtue will ripen. You will follow your guru.
His intentions will be fulfilled.
The disciple will achieve the guru's liberation.

And from the *Tantra of the Array of Ati*:

Whoever unmistakenly calculates
The year, month, and day of their guru's passing
And presents offerings at that time
Will complete the two accumulations.[117]
Their wealth will increase in this life.

Sharawa said:

Among all composite virtue the most meritorious is the presentation of offerings upon the passing of one's spiritual friend.

117. This refers both to the presentation of elaborate offerings immediately after the guru's passing and to the presentation of offerings on the anniversary of his passing.

This is extolled in countless sutras, tantras, and upadeshas. If you enthusiastically follow your glorious guru's example by recollecting all of the qualities of his three secrets and all of his kindness; praying to him with strong faith, devotion, and yearning; presenting offerings and praise; and especially accomplishing his instructions, you will definitely achieve the supreme siddhi of mahamudra in this life and become of one taste with the wisdom of your guru, Mahavajradhara.

I have written this brief biography of our guru with the motivation of faith and devotion. I repeatedly asked our supreme guru to dictate a brief autobiography, but he always refused, saying, "I am an ordinary person. There is nothing I could tell you about my life that would inspire faith in others."

Nevertheless Rinpoche has spoken of his life in bits and pieces in response to the questions of disciples and in the context of conversation. I have not let what he has said about his life go to waste. I have also not exaggerated anything. I have written down everything he has said exactly as he said it, without alteration.

In writing my guru's biography, my aim has been to increase the devotion of myself and others by revealing the deeds and state of this supreme guru whose kindness to me exceeds that of anyone else. Also it is the responsibility of a disciple to record the deeds of their guru. I have for many years been seated at the end of the rows of his disciples and am nominally his attendant. Our guru's deeds and compassion are so great that the wider their proclamation, the more devotion there will be. I have written this while rejoicing in his deeds and state, not out of the need to flatter my uncle or claim his superiority to others. I am not motivated by family pride or by the inappropriate desire to exaggerate his qualities because he is my guru. Although I lack even a sesame seed's worth of the qualities of learning and realization that would make me worthy of being his disciple, I delight in unremitting honesty. Cast far away any doubts as to the truth of what I have written.

You may be thinking, "Is it appropriate for a disciple to write their guru's biography without their guru's permission?" Thrangu Khenpo Trinlay Palzang wrote me a letter in which he asked me to write our guru's biography. Kyapjay Lodrö Nyima Rinpoche also encouraged me to do so. I started to write it, but still lacked Khenpo Rinpoche's permission to publish it. So I said to him, "Although you have not dictated an autobiography to me, others have encouraged me to write about your life. Would it be acceptable for me to write a brief account of your life based on what you have told me and emphasizing the greatness of the Sixteenth Gyalwang Karmapa?"

He was silent for a while. After thinking it over, Rinpoche said, "Well, it's up to you."

With, therefore, his permission, I, a monk from Thrangu Monastery named Karma Drodül, the nephew of this holy being and the least of his disciples, have auspiciously completed this during my second retreat at the glorious Gyalwang Karmapa's retreat center Yiwong Samten Ling in the United States of America on the 29th of November, 2005, the Tibetan Year 2132 of the Wood Bird, while engaged in the inner sadhana of Vajravarahi.

Rinpoche and Bardor Tulku Rinpoche with His Holiness the Seventeenth Gyalwang Karmapa, Karma Thegsum Chöling, New Jersey, 2008.

Karme Ling Retreat Center, 2002.
From left, clockwise: Pawo Ling, Kandro Ling, Ani House, Lama House. The photo-
graph does not include the columbarium, situated in the open space to the right of
Kandro Ling, and the new individual retreat cabins found to the left of Pawo Ling.

Part Three
Virtue in the End

Rinpoche and Bardor Tulku Rinpoche, Karme Ling Retreat Center while under construction, ca. 1991.

Longevity Supplications, Dedications, and Aspirations

With the Sixteenth Gyalwang Karmapa, Dawes Arboretum, Ohio, 1980.

True Words of Longevity

You've completed the path of the two
    accumulations over many kalpas
And achieved its result, the dharmakaya.
You are peerless, wondrous, and glorious. Your
    qualities are infinite.
Victors of the three times, bestow virtue and
    goodness!

With unfabricated faith you obey your guru's
    commands.
The good vase of your heart is filled with the
    amrita of scripture and reasoning.
You are constantly and devotedly diligent in
    teaching and accomplishment.
Holy being who raises up the Victor's teachings,
I pray that you remain.

You light the beacon of dharma in a land where it
    was previously absent.
You bring happiness to the minds of all kinds
    of beings.

You are always on the path of nonviolence,
   peace, and happiness.
Holy being with flawless morality, I pray that
   you remain.

Through my stainlessly pure and virtuous
   intentions;
And through my unfailing, good, and strong
   aspirations,
May the good result I wish for be quickly
   achieved.
May we all be filled with the light of goodness.

This supplication for the longevity of Khenpo Karthar
Rinpoche was written directly at the earnest request of his
disciples by Ogyen Trinley Palden Wangi Dorje, holder of
the name Karmapa, on April 6th, 2002 at the Upper
Tantric University in India. SHUBHAM!

A Prayer for the Longevity of Khenpo Karthar Rinpoche

Three jewels, through your wisdom and love
   for all beings
You reach every realm with your dance
Of countless and endless emanations.
Compassionately cause this holder of the
   teachings to live long.

So that every being in this difficult time
May be brought to liberation, the four bodies,
May this ceaseless turner of the three yanas'
   dharmachakras,
This holder of the teachings, live long.

From spiritual friends, the scions of the three
   times' victors,
He learned every aspect of the dharma of sutra
   and mantra.
His life is an example of brilliance and vigor.
May this spiritual friend of the supreme yana
   live long.

The teachings of our guide, Shakyamuni, both
    tradition and realization,
Have been upheld by many scholars and siddhas
    of India and Tibet.
This holy being effortlessly bestows them upon
    disciples at the right time.
May he live long.

On the unshakable mountain of the three jewels'
    compassion
May this lion among spiritual friends be ever
    vigorous.
May he fill this world with his roar, the dharma of
    tradition and realization.
May there be the auspicious four joys of a
    golden age.

Disciples of the holy holder of the teachings, Khenpo
Karthar Rinpoche, requested a prayer for his longevity. In
response, this was written by the Jikdral Dakchen of the
glorious Sakyas on February 4th, 2008. May virtue and
goodness increase!

Longevity Prayer and Aspiration

NAMO Through the blessing of the truth of the gurus, buddhas,
Dharma, and sangha — the three jewels and three roots —
May the Victor's teachings flourish and long remain.
May all beings be perfectly happy.

Especially, may the holy beings who hold the teachings live long.
May their deeds and activity be complete.
May the essence of the lineage of Shakyamuni's dharma last
Until the future appearance of Maitreya's teachings.

Indefatigable in bearing the heavy burden of all the teachings
And especially those of the accomplishment lineage,
May the learned and accomplished Karma Tarchin live long.

May his excellent deeds be spontaneously
   successful.

Through the blessing of the infallible, holy sources
   of refuge;
And through the powerful truth of pure dharmata,
May these, my words of benevolent aspiration,
Be fulfilled as I intend.

At the request of disciples from Karma Triyana
Dharmachakra, the Gyalwang Karmapa's seat in
America, and from its affiliated Karma Thegsum
Chöling centers, these words of longevity prayer and
aspiration were written by Kenting Tai Situpa. May they
be accomplished!

May Virtue and Excellence Increase!

The precious hub of your meditation is utterly
   stable.
The thousand jeweled spokes of your wisdom
   flash in every direction.
You have the golden rim of pure morality.
I pray that Karma Tarchin live for a hundred
   kalpas.

At the request of Raymond Wu, this was written by
Jamgön Kongtrul Lodrö Chökyi Nyima on the 27th of
December, 2007, at Vajrasana, the best of places. May
virtue and excellence increase!

Khenpo Rinpoche's birthday celebration, Karma Triyana
Dharmachakra, ca. 1986-87.

Longevity Aspiration

Through the blessings of all victors'
compassion
And the power of our purely good intentions
May this completer of the activity
Of the glorious Gyalwang Karmapa live long.

At the request of Khenpo Rinpoche's disciples, this was
written by one called Thrangu Tulku. Virtue!

Karma Triyana Dharmachakra, 1980s.

Longevity Prayer

Karma, perfect expanse of the victors' stainless
compassion,
Lord of the eighty marks and signs, source of
countless joys,
Sun that nourishes the lotus garden of beings
and the teachings:
Remain in this world amid the millionfold
auspicious joy and goodness of your peerless
activity.

In celebration of the peerlessly kind Khenpo Karthar
Rinpoche's achievement of the age of eighty, his disciple
Raymond Wu requested words of auspiciousness and
aspiration. This was therefore written by Lodrö Nyima at
the Thrangu Dharma Center in Hong Kong. Virtue!

Tendzin Chönyi, Khenpo Karthar Rinpoche, Bardor Tulku Rinpoche, Chögyam Trungpa Rinpoche, and Lama Yeshe Losal, Karma Triyana Dharmachakra, 1979.

Longevity Prayer for Khenpo Kárthar Rinpoche

O M SVASTI Karmapa is the life-tree of the accomplishment lineage's teachings. You courageously expand his activity to the ends of space in every direction. May you live long in the nature of the three vajras. May you spontaneously accomplish the completion of your deeds.[118]

At the request of his disciples in the Sönam Gyamtso Association, who said, "We need a longevity prayer for Khenpo Karthar Rinpoche," this was written at Kagyu Thubten Chöling by Lama Norlha. May virtue and goodness increase!

118. The three vajras are the pure body, speech, and mind of an awakened being. "Completion" here is a play on Khenpo Rinpoche's name, Karma Tarchin, because Tarchin can mean "completion." Most longevity supplications include in their words the name of the master for whose longevity one is praying.

Family Dharma Weekend, Heart Center, Karma Thegsum Chöling, near Big Rapids, Michigan, 1987.

This concludes a brief but inspiring outer biography of our great guide, our kind guru whose deeds on behalf of the accomplishment lineage are unsurpassable, and a collection of prayers for his longevity.

This biography of our glorious guru of twelvefold
    greatness
Is the indispensable inheritance of the devoted
    who seek liberation.
The realization through reductive reasoning of
    primordially present wisdom
And many kalpas' collection of the accumulations
    are perfected just by devotion to the guru.

Through the virtue of writing this may the
    glorious guru,
The lord of dharma, the great guide of beings and
    the teachings,
Live as long as the deities of life so that he may
Lead me and all his disciples on the path to
    liberation.

With Dr. Shen, Chuang Yen Monastery, Carmel, New York, 2007.

I confess to the threefold guru
My beginningless accumulation of bad karma
and veils,
And especially all violations of the three vows.
See me from the expanse of nonreferential
compassion!

In this life and all future lives
May I never be separated from the glorious guru.
In the delightful, auspicious garden of dharma
May we all, master and disciples, attain
buddhahood together.

This lacks the elegant composition and poetry
that pleases the learned.
It is without the quotations and reasoning that
please the intelligent.
However, may it cause blessings to be transferred
to the hearts
Of those who delight in the path of devotion.

May the great holders of the undivided teachings
live long.
May our parents, all beings in the six states,
objects of our undivided love,
Be nourished by the undivided holy dharma
And realize the undivided, primordially present
wisdom.

SARVA MANGALAM!

Thrangu Rinpoche, Traleg Rinpoche, and Khenpo Rinpoche, during Thrangu Rinpoche's visit to Karma Triyana Dharmachakra, 2002.

Karma Triyana Dharmachakra

Karma Triyana Dharmachakra (KTD) is the North American seat of His Holiness the Gyalwang Karmapa, and under the spiritual guidance and protection of His Holiness Ogyen Trinley Dorje, the Seventeenth Gyalwang Karmapa, is devoted to the authentic representation of the Kagyu lineage of Tibetan Buddhism.

For information regarding KTD, including our current schedule, or for information regarding our affiliate centers, Karma Thegsum Chöling (KTCs), located both in the United States and internationally, contact us using the information below. If you would like to make a donation to KTD, contact Development.

Karma Triyana Dharmachakra
335 Meads Mountain Road
Woodstock, NY, 12498 USA
845 679 5906 ext. 10
www.kagyu.org
Development: 845 679 5906 ext. 38
development@kagyu.org
KTC Coordinator: 845 679 5906 ext. 44
ktc@kagyu.org

The four tulkus of Thrangu Monastery: the previous (Eighth) Khenchen Thrangu Rinpoche, the previous (Eighth) Traleg Kyabgön Rinpoche, the previous (Eighth) Lodrö Nyima Rinpoche, and the previous (Sixth) Zuru Tulku Rinpoche, Thrangu Monastery, Kham, East Tibet, 1922.

Thrangu Tashi Chöling Monastery

Thrangu Tashi Chöling Monastery, located near Jekundo on a high plateau in East Tibet, was founded by the Seventh Karmapa Chödrak Gyamtso (1454-1506) in the fifteenth century. He enthroned Sherap Gyaltsen, the First Thrangu Rinpoche, as abbot, recognizing him as the reincarnation of Guru Rinpoche's heart son Shubu Palgyi Sengey.

There are four incarnate tulkus of Thrangu Tashi Chöling: Traleg Kyabgön Rinpoche, Khenchen Thrangu Rinpoche, Lodrö Nyima Rinpoche, and Zuru Tulku Rinpoche. Today the monastery continues with its reconstruction and growth after the 1959 invasion.

This is the monastery where Khenpo Karthar Rinpoche was until 1959; he continues to serve Thrangu Monastery in addition to serving Karma Triyana Dharmachakra.

E-mail address : lodroenyima@gmail.com
Tel : +86 976 882-3190 / 882-5671
Fax : +86 976 882-8106

His Holiness the Seventeenth Gyalwang Karmapa visits the columbarium at Karme Ling Retreat Center, Delhi, New York, 2008.

Karme Ling Retreat Center

Karme Ling Retreat Center is a traditional three-year retreat center associated with Karma Triyana Dharmachakra. Opened in 1992, Karme Ling is located in the rolling hills outside of Delhi, New York. Since then, retreats have been completed every four years, and retreat graduates are now teaching in dharma centers around the world.

For information about the traditional three-year retreat or to send donations to support the retreat, please contact:

Karme Ling Retreat Center
315 Retreat Road
Delhi, NY 13753
karmeling@kagyu.org

KTD Publications

Gathering the garlands of the gurus' precious teachings

KTD Publications, a part of Karma Triyana Dharmachakra, is a not-for-profit publisher established with the purpose of facilitating the projects and activities manifesting from His Holiness Karmapa's inspiration and blessings. We are dedicated to gathering the garlands of precious teachings and producing fine-quality books.

We invite you to join KTD Publications in facilitating the activities of His Holiness Karmapa and fulfilling the wishes of Khenpo Karthar Rinpoche and Bardor Tulku Rinpoche. If you would like to sponsor a book or make a donation to KTD Publications, please contact us using the information below. All contributions are tax deductible.

KTD Publications
335 Meads Mountain Road
Woodstock, NY 12498 USA
Telephone: 845 679 5906 ext. 37
maureen@ktdpublications.org
www.KTDPublications.org

Books by Khenpo Karthar Rinpoche

The Quintessence of the Union of Mahamudra and Dzokchen, by Karma Chakme Rinpoche, translated by Yeshe Gyamtso, root text translated by Peter Alan Roberts, KTD Publications, 2007

Bardo: Interval of Possibility: Khenpo Karthar Rinpoche's Commentary on Aspiration for the Bardo by Chökyi Wangchuk, translated by Yeshe Gyamtso, KTD Publications, 2007

Karma Chakme's Mountain Dharma as Taught by Khenpo Karthar Rinpoche: *Volume One*, 2004; *Volume Two*, 2006; *Volume Three*, 2008; *Volumes Four* and *Five*, 2009; translated by Yeshe Gyamtso, Chökyong Radha, and Namgyal Khorko, KTD Publications

The Wish-Fulfilling Wheel: The Practice of White Tara by Khenpo Karthar Rinpoche, Rinchen Publications, 2003 (also in Chinese)

The Instructions of Gampopa: A Precious Garland of the Supreme Path, translated by Lama Yeshe Gyamtso, Snow Lion Publications, 1996

Dharma Paths, Snow Lion Publications, 1993

Forthcoming Titles:

Kham Masters, as told by Khenpo Karthar Rinpoche to Lama Karma Drodül, translated by Lama Yeshe Gyamtso

Stories Told by Khenpo Rinpoche, photographs and stories, KTD Publications

The Essence of the Union of Mahamudra and Dzokchen, by Karma Chakme Rinpoche, Four Volumes, translated by Yeshe Gyamtso, KTD Publications

Lamp of Mahamudra, by Tsele Natsok Rangdrol, translated by Yeshe Gyamtso, KTD Publications

Gampopa's Community Letters, translated by Yeshe Gyamtso, KTD Publications

May All Beings Be Happy